ELVIS

ELVIS

K.D. KIRKLAND
with a preface by
SANDY MARTINDALE

LONGMEADOW PRESS

Copyright © 1988 by Brompton Books Corporation

Published by Longmeadow Press, 201 High Ridge Road, Stamford, CT 06904. All rights reserved. No part of this book may be reproduced or utilized in any form or by any means, electronic or mechanical, including photocopying, recording or by any information storage and retrieval system, without permission in writing from the Publisher.

Longmeadow Press and the colophon are registered trademarks.

ISBN 0-681-00575-0

Printed in China

First Longmeadow Press Edition

0 9 8 7 6 5 4 3 2

TABLE OF CONTENTS

Preface 6
Part 1 The Hillbilly Cat 8
Part 2 The GI Years 28
Part 3 The Hollywood Years ... 34
Part 4 His Private Life 64
Part 5 Las Vegas to Graceland . 72
Part 6 The King Remembered .. 88
Index 108

Preface

I first met Elvis Aron Presley on Thursday, 21 April 1960, at my father's nightclub, The Crossbow. He had to come to Los Angeles to make the movie *GI Blues*, which was released the following November.

I loved Elvis for most of my life. When I was with him and when he held me in his arms, I felt so complete that even if the world had come to an end at that moment it would have been okay with me. I can't remember ever feeling more secure. The day he died, a part of me died. This year I will be 42, the age at which Elvis left us, but he will always be with me in spirit and love.

Those of us who were lucky enough to have had their lives touched by Elvis are truly blessed. To have experienced the excitement of his presence in a room was electrifying. So was the joy of his infectious laugh, his magnetic crooked smile, and the fun of his devilish, little-boy pranks. He was capable of great sensitivity, friendship and love.

Elvis was a truly compassionate man, and I think his manner was influenced by his surroundings and the people around him. If someone was polite and kind, he was polite and kind. If they were not, he would meet them on their own level. He tried to make people feel at home with him. He was more vulnerable than he knew, which I feel is one of the reasons he is no longer with us.

I am extremely lucky! I am happily married to another Tennessee boy—Wink Martindale—who makes me feel as secure and complete as Elvis ever did. I once told Elvis that he was responsible for me having fallen in love with a man from Tennessee. Wink had, in fact, been a good friend of Elvis before I met either of them, and he was on the air at WHBQ Radio in Memphis on the night that Elvis was 'discovered.'

Elvis was a wonderful man and a true gentleman. He was special and he *is* special; he will always live on in our hearts. There is no way to measure the fun that we had and the love and friendship that we all shared. We miss him terribly! We will always have our memories of this very special man. He gave us all he had to give.

Sandy

Sandra L Martindale

Wink and Sandy today.

ELVIS The Hillbilly Cat

In 1934, 18-year-old Vernon Elvis Presley borrowed $180 for materials to build a small frame house for himself and his 22-year old bride, Gladys Love Presley, in East Tupelo, Mississippi. It was the height of the Great Depression and work was as hard to find as it was to keep. Vernon alternately farmed cotton, did house painting, and worked as a WPA carpenter. He worked on his own home when he could find time.

At 12:20 pm, on 8 January 1935, Gladys gave birth to twins—Elvis Aron* and Jesse Garon. Six hours later, little Jesse was dead, but his brother went on to live a life like no other. Tradition has it that when one twin dies, the other grows up with all the qualities of the other; perhaps this is why Elvis Presley found himself doubly endowed with talents and energies beyond the range of common men.

One of Elvis' first memories was that of being hungry. He remembered his father sobbing because he couldn't pay all their bills, and his mother sacrificing to help to get through the tough times. His mother worked in a dress factory and his father would occasionally get part time truck driving jobs.

Times were rough, but the Presley family survived in relative happiness—almost on faith alone. Each Sunday they would attend the Fundamentalist Assembly of God Church on Adams Street in Tupelo, about half a mile from their home. Today that church still stands, and is known as the East Heights Assembly of God Church.

Elvis looked forward to churchgoing on Sundays; there he could sing as loud as he wanted to. Music in the Presleys' Fundamentalist church had its roots in black spirituals; everyone joined in 'raising the roof,' and this was to be a big influence on Elvis' own music. In October 1946, when he was still at Lawhan Grade School, his fifth grade teacher, Mrs Grames, entered him in a talent contest at the Mississippi-Alabama Fair and Dairy show, where he won second place and five dollars singing the ballad 'Old Shep.' Broadcast over WELO radio, this was Elvis' first public solo performance. No recordings of it are known to exist.

---

* His middle name was originally officially recorded as being spelled with one 'a' although it has been frequently seen with the conventional spelling, Aaron. The latter is, in fact, used on his gravestone.

Elvis was born in this small frame house *(below)*, which his father built in Tupelo, Mississippi. Though his twin brother Jesse survived just a few hours in this world, Elvis went on to conquer it. *At right* is the kitchen of the house, in which Elvis was nourished through his boyhood.

At right and below: His earliest memories were in this room, of this wallpaper, beyond this mirror, beneath this sky. Note the photo of Elvis, Vernon and Gladys, taken in about 1937 when Elvis was two.

The Presleys had lost their house early on, when Vernon could not keep up the payments on it. But until Elvis was ready for high school, the family stayed in Tupelo. In September 1948, however, they moved to the 'big town' of Memphis, where Vernon felt he had a better chance of finding steady work. In Memphis, the Presleys settled into a two-bedroom house at 572 Poplar Avenue. Elvis apparently found it hard to make friends in his new surroundings and spent many hours in solitude. The time alone, however, was not spent unproductively, because he had a $12.95 guitar that his dad had given him for his eleventh birthday. The Tupelo Hardware Store, where this first guitar was purchased, still stands.

When Elvis attended O C Hume High School in Memphis, he was on his own, musically *and* socially. He found it difficult to make friends and confessed later that 'The girls didn't go for me then.' Although he went out for both football and baseball, he did not make either team.

Elvis was never a particularly good student and shop classes were his favorites. For a while he enrolled in the high school ROTC program but did not continue for very long. After school and on weekends he worked as a movie attendant at Lowes State Theater and swept floors at Marx Metal Products. At age 16 he adopted sideburns and a 'ducktail' haircut while most everyone else was wearing crewcuts. He wanted to be different, to look older and, of course, to be noticed. He later took to wearing black clothes and this, in conjunction

11

with the sideburns, gave him the difference he needed to stand out in a crowd.

After the 'Old Shep' performance in 1946, Elvis next performed before an audience in March 1953 near the end of his senior year at Hume. He appeared at the high school's variety show and performed four songs ranging from plaintive ballads to more up-tempo numbers. Witnesses remember that these two musical styles were alternated during the performance, ending with a particularly fast song that sent the audience into near hysteria. Although it is difficult to isolate exactly where the Elvis legend began, this variety show concert generally serves to mark beginning of an entertainment style that would literally rock the world for the next quarter century.

After the show Elvis suddenly found himself quite a popular figure at Hume, cutting a dashing figure as he strode about with his cheap guitar slung over his shoulder most of the time.

Following his graduation, Elvis worked the graveyard shift in a factory. It was at this time that Vernon Presley injured his back and could no longer work for extended periods, so Elvis' mother went to work in a hospital making beds and scrubbing floors. As time went on, however, his mother's health began to fail and his father's back injury worsened so that it became difficult for him to even walk.

Elvis himself began to feel helpless. He was only 18 and barely out of high school when the realization came to him that he was now a grown man, and that his parents' future really depended on him and on whatever he could make of his life. He hoped and prayed he would eventually be able to help with more than the $35 he was now making each week as a truck driver for the Crown Electric Company. Elvis recalled that he got down on his knees and prayed to God to show him some way to help his parents. Heaven was listening that day!

His mother's birthday was approaching and Elvis was trying to think of something to cheer her up. As he was driving the Crown Electric truck down the main street in Memphis he noticed a sign which read: *'Memphis Recording Services.'* He had his guitar in the back of the truck, so he stopped in to check things out. Apparently Sun Records offered a recording service to anyone willing to pay a four dollar fee. Some of the studio personnel remember Elvis looking like a drifter wanting a handout, but he paid his money and recorded two songs, 'My Happiness' and 'That's When Your Heartache Begins,' figuring the idea of having his voice professionally recorded

These pages: **The 'Hillbilly Cat' during one of his earliest recording sessions. Captured on tape, they remain raw, unadulterated dynamite!**

would tickle his mother. Elvis thought his performance was horrible, that his guitar was out of tune, and that his voice cracked. It was the first time he had ever heard himself sing.

He returned to Sun Records in January 1954 to make a second record. This time the ten-inch disk contained 'Casual Love Affair' an 'I'll Never Stand in Your Way.' This time, Sam Phillips, head of Memphis Recording Services, as well as the Sun Record Company, heard the recordings—and he liked what he heard! In July, he sent Elvis to work with Scotty Moore and Bill Blake, both talented, well-known musicians. With Moore on guitar, Blake on bass and Elvis on both guitar and vocals, the trio rehearsed for two days and cut 'Blue Moon of Kentucky,' 'Harbor Lights,' 'Just Because,' 'I Love You Because,' 'I'll Never Let You Go,' and 'That's Alright, Mama.' Phillips took the latter track, which was a mixture of jazz and country music, to a disc jockey, Dewey Phillips, who, on the following day—7 July 1954—played it on his night-time radio program on WHBQ. The audience response was immediate. Phones at the radio station began ringing off their hooks. (Wink Martindale, eventually one of Elvis' best friends, was also working at WHBQ that night.)

On 19 July Sam Phillips signed Elvis to a three-year contract with the Sun Records label, which at that time was also the venue for the work of such future greats as Johnny Cash, Jerry Lee Lewis and Carl Perkins. 'That's Alright, Mama' b/w 'Blue Moon of Kentucky' was the first release. Within a week, 7000 copies of 'That's Alright, Mama' were sold in Memphis, and eventually Sun sold 20,000.

On July 30, Elvis opened for Slim Whitman at a Memphis concert. In September, along with Scotty Moore and Bill Blake, he went back into the Sun studio to record his second record—'I Don't Care if the Sun Don't Shine' b/w 'Good Rockin' Tonight.' On 25 September Elvis travelled to Nashville for what was to be his only appearance on the *Grand Ole Opry*. Despite having been voted 'Most Promising New Artist of the Year' by *Billboard* magazine, Elvis was greeted with a chilly reception from the *Opry*, the same institution which, in its infinite creative wisdom, had fired Hank Williams on 11 August 1952, barely two years earlier.

The following month, however, Elvis was hired by another variety show, the Shreveport-based *Louisiana Hayride*, for which he made his first appearance on 16 October. With a nearly six-fold increase in pay, Elvis was at last able to quit his job at Crown Electric to go forth and electrify the youth of Tennessee, the South, and eventually the world.

His first step toward world-class stardom came on 1 January 1955, when he signed a contract with Bob Neal, a local disc jockey, for a six-month series of one-night stands through Texas, Arkansas and Louisiana. The bobby-soxers loved his bumping and grinding as much as the music, and the tour propelled the teenager now known as the 'Hillbilly Cat' into being more than just a local Memphis sensation, although his records would not receive any airplay outside the South until the fall of 1955. In the meantime, Elvis recorded a number of other songs for Sun including 'Mystery Train' and 'Baby, Let's Play House' which are regarded as major highlights of his early career.

In March 1955 Elvis made his television debut in a regionally televised *Louisiana Hayride*, but the following month, he was turned down in an audition for Arthur Godfrey's *Talent Scouts*.

Elvis' last appearance on the *Hayride* would come on 17 December, and from there, the sky would be the limit.

In November 1955, RCA Victor bought his Sun recording

Carl Perkins *(at top, above)* wrote 'Blue Suede Shoes,' which Elvis later recorded and used in his stage shows. *Above, left to right:* Jerry Lee Lewis, Carl Perkins, Elvis and Johnny Cash gather around a piano at the Sun studios. *At right:* Elvis, a rising star in the mid-1950s.

contract and five master discs for $35,000, which was, for that time, an unheard-of sum. (Columbia had offered $15,000 and Atlantic $25,000). Elvis was even given a bonus of $5000 to cover future royalties, which he promptly spent on a Cadillac—his first, but certainly not his last!

January 1956 found the 'Hillbilly Cat' in RCA's Nashville studios laying down his first tracks for the company that would remain his home for the rest of his career. His first RCA session included Ray Charles' 'I Got a Woman,' 'Money Honey' and his legendary 'Heartbreak Hotel,' one of the songs for which he is best remembered.

At the end of January, Elvis went north to RCA's New York studios, where he recorded another group of tracks which remain enshrined today as Elvis classics. Among them were 'Lawdy Miss Clawdy,' 'Shake, Rattle and Roll,' Little Richard's 'Tutti Frutti,' and 'Blue Suede Shoes,' a song penned by Carl Perkins, a fellow Sun Records alumnus.

Elvis went on to do several recording sessions—some say his greatest sessions—during 1956. Among the three dozen tracks that were laid down in New York, Nashville and Los Angeles were such classics as 'Don't Be Cruel,' 'Ready Teddy,' 'Rip it Up,' 'Long Tall Sally' and a remake of 'Old Shep,' which he had sung at his first public appearance a long decade before. Among the treasure-trove of hits that he put on tape during his 2 July 1956 session in New York was the song which is regarded as his all time greatest hit: '(You Ain't Nothin' But a) Hound Dog.'

At this time RCA was the largest recording company in America, with an enormous output of records, and a tremendous range of talent. Yet within three months of his initial contract signing with the company, Elvis' recordings accounted

At left, **Live in Shreveport:** 'You ain't nothin' but a hound dog and you ain't no friend of mine.' But they *were,* Elvis, millions of them! This photo was taken during the *Louisiana Hayride* in 1955, before he joined RCA. *Below left:* **The hottest Rock n' Roller in the USA in his dressing room…and on the floor were his blue suede shoes.** *Below:* **Mail call for the top US male, circa 1956.**

for more than half of RCA's sales. By the end of 1956, RCA had grossed almost seven million dollars on Elvis products.

It is interesting to note that in the studio, Elvis liked to go slowly and meticulously. Sometimes he would take two or three days to get the sound he wanted, but his popularity and profitability more than outweighed the recording executives' frustrations. Elvis recorded his music with a care and a precision which can still be sensed when listening to it today. Somehow he felt he was singing into history and he was right. Those notes and harmonies were, and will be, imprinted on the hearts and minds of not only his own generation, but also on those of generations into the foreseeable future.

While he was in New York, Elvis signed to perform on the nationally televised Dorsey Brothers *Stage Show.* In six appearances between 28 January and 24 March 1956, he gained far more in terms of exposure than could be measured from the $7500 he was paid for the appearances. He was no longer a Memphis celebrity, nor even just a southern celebrity—the 20-year-old 'Hillbilly Cat' was now a national star!

In the first week of April, he was paid $5000 for a *single* appearance on the *Milton Berle Show*, was reviewed in the *New York Times* and was signed by Hal Wallis of Paramount in Hollywood to a $450,000 contract to appear in three movies!

In the meantime, on 15 March, Elvis had signed a new manager—Colonel Tom Parker. The Colonel met Elvis while he was on tour in July 1955, and was immediately impressed with his mannerisms and the easy way in which he accepted constructive criticism and direction.

Parker realized there was a certain magic in the almost contradictory nature of Elvis on and off stage. On stage he was often raunchy, grinding and sensual; off stage, however, he was a humble and polite Southern gentleman who always said 'Yes, Ma'am' and 'No, Sir.' Colonel Parker once said of Elvis, 'When I met him he only had a million dollars worth of talent, now he has a million dollars!' Parker remained Elvis' business manager almost until Elvis' death in 1977.

Parker was an entrepreneur of the first magnitude. He knew that this singing version of James Dean was in fact the Frank Sinatra of his generation, and he stayed up nights developing ways to promote him; most of which were historically successful. Elvis always believed that he and the Colonel were good for each other.

Parker was in fact an honorary 'Colonel,' the title having been bestowed upon him by the legendary governor of Louisiana, the 'Kingfish' Huey Long, who was struck down by an assassin's bullet the year that Elvis was born. Parker at one time promoted Hadacol, a patent medicine. It was Parker who brought Elvis national recognition—on the Milton Berle, Steve Allen, Jackie Gleason and Ed Sullivan variety shows. When the two first met, Elvis' personal appearance fee was $200, but Parker soon raised it to $5000—and more!

Parker also set up a merchandising plan which flooded the country with Elvis Presley products. Of course, the Colonel received a percentage of the box office profits and the royalties from performances and songs. Some rumors pegged his take as being as much as 50 percent of Elvis' earnings.

With great fame always comes an equal amount of criticism. Most parents in the 1950s simply were not ready for 'all that sinful shakin'.' Elvis refused to tone down his act even though Colonel Parker and others strongly advised him to do so. When he appeared on Ed Sullivan's *Toast of the Town* show, in September 1956, his hip grinding antics were thought to be too sexually provocative and the cameramen

Above: **Elvis on the drums. He recorded his music with care and precision, and he worked meticulously.** ***Below:*** **At the piano.** ***At right:*** **Charisma you could fry eggs with! He gave it all he had.**

were instructed to use tight shots of his guitar, shoulders and head and thus avoid those palpitating hips. Elvis fumed at the censorship and threatened to never submit to it again. But public morality was on the line, and so another method had to be found—to both control Elvis' act and, at the same time, project him into the consciousness of the millions of fans who longed to see his every move. Movies were the answer.

When Hal Wallis, a Hollywood movie producer, saw one of Elvis' TV appearances he thought he saw 'a new Marlon Brando.' He signed Elvis to a contract. In 1956, Elvis had earned his first million dollars, and he was to repeat this accomplishment many times over—every year for the rest of his life. But with this first movie contract, Elvis embarked on a new career.

Elvis' original movie contract was to have been with Paramount Studios, but since Paramount had no immediate use for his talents, he was loaned out to 20th Century Fox. His first film, which began shooting on 22 August 1956, was a western originally titled *The Reno Brothers*. Before its release, however, the title was changed to *Love Me Tender* to match one of the four songs that Elvis was recording for the film's soundtrack. It was completed in a matter of weeks and was released on 16 November.

Receiving top billing in the film were Richard Egan, who portrayed Vance Reno, the oldest of the four brothers for whom the film was originally to have been named, and Deborah Paget, who played Cathy, the romantic interest. Elvis played Clint Reno, the youngest of brothers, and the one who stays on the family farm in Texas while the older Renos leave to fight with the Confederate States in the Civil War. Clint has always been in love with Cathy, who has inconveniently been

Above: *Love Me Tender*—with Deborah Paget—his first film. The title song had women from 18 to 80 weeping in their theater seats. *At right:* The Hillbilly Cat adjusts his coiffure, ready for stardom.

the sweetheart of his brother, Vance. When news arrives that Vance has been killed, Clint woos and marries her. However, Vance is not actually dead, so when he returns, a feud naturally arises between the brothers, ending in Clint's death.

In the film, when Elvis paused from his fussin' and fightin' to sing 'Love Me Tender,' 'Poor Boy,' 'We're Gonna Move,' and 'Let Me,' fans responded as if it were a live concert. Near hysteria took over when Elvis planted his first screen kiss on Deborah Paget. Never before, nor since, has such audience reaction to a film been witnessed. It still remains one of the most popular films Hollywood ever produced.

Originally, Elvis had taught himself how to sing and in his Hollywood career, he would also teach himself how to act. Just as he had listened to many records over and over in order to teach himself vocal harmonics, so he would view many, many films hoping to catch the secrets of such stars as Marlon Brando and James Dean. He wanted to be a good actor and thought he could do it. He felt that all he had to do was really try and put his heart into it.

The endearing personality of the 'Hillbilly Cat' from the Mississippi hills took Hollywood by storm. His co-workers spoke highly of his polite manner, perceiving him as both eager and humble, so that most everyone went out of his or her way to help him.

In September 1956, Elvis interrupted his picture-making schedule to perform at a homecoming celebration at the Mississippi-Alabama Fair in Tupelo, the same venue where he had won five dollars for his rendition of 'Old Shep' 10 years earlier. This time, over 20,000 people, mostly teenagers, almost ransacked the town. Not wanting to miss out on an opportunity, local restaurants served 'Love Me Tender' steaks, 'Hound Dogs' and 'Ooby Dooby' cakes with 'Tutti Frutti' sauce. Elvis recalled that as a child he did not have the 25 cent admission to get into the fair, so he sneaked in over the fence. He was escorted out—now he was being escorted in! He gave two performances and made over $10,000.

Early in 1957, Elvis began work on his second film. This time he would receive top billing and the title—*Loving You*—was taken directly from one of his songs, recorded in Hollywood in February. The film was, in fact, vaguely autobiographical insofar as Elvis played Deke Rivers, a poor country boy who joined a travelling hillbilly band and sang his way to success. Besides 'Loving You,' Elvis recorded six additional songs—'Hot Dog,' 'Lonesome Cowboy,' 'Got a Lot of Livin' to Do,' 'Let's Have a Party,' 'Detour' and 'Dancing on the Dare'—for the soundtrack. Directed by Hal Kanter and produced by Hal Wallis for Paramount Pictures, the film's unlisted credits included the now-ubiquitous Colonel Parker as

At left: Elvis' real band, the Jordanaires, back his character in *Loving You*. Susan (Dolores Hart), *above and below,* was Deke Rivers' (Elvis) sweet and wholesome downhome girlfriend, while Glenda (Lizbeth Scott), *at right*, was a spike-heeled ambitious publicist.

24

'Technical Advisor.' Released on 9 July 1957, *Loving You* co-starred Lizabeth Scott, Wendell Corey, Delores Hart and James Gleason.

In May 1957, even before *Loving You* was released, Elvis began work on his third movie in less than a year! Now the medium was considered a major showcase for his talent. *Jailhouse Rock* was unusual because Elvis' role called for him to appear self-centered and mean throughout much of the film. This 'tough-guy' lead was the role of Vince Everett, a young man who, while trying to defend a lady, kills a man. While behind bars for manslaughter, Vince is taught by a cell mate to sing and play the guitar. In the course of his evolution from punk to rocker, Vince performs the spectacular song and dance number (choreographed by Elvis himself) to the film's title song which remains a hallmark of Elvis Presley's early career.

When Vince gets out of stir he forms a recording company called Laurel Records. Fame and money become his heritage and he turns into a conceited millionaire. Among the songs that Elvis performed in the guise of Vince Everett are 'Young and Beautiful,' 'I Want to be Free,' 'Don't Leave Me Now,' 'Treat Me Nice,' and '(You're So Square) I Don't Care.'

Ultimately, thanks to the advice of co-star Dean Jones and romantic interest Judy Tyler, Vince Everett evolves into a nice

At left: Elvis, doing time as the courageous, but mean and egotistical Vince Everett, in *Jailhouse Rock*. *At top, above* is the fight scene in which Vince commits manslaughter. He then is arrested and is remanded to prison *(above)*—which turns out to be a good break.

guy and *Jailhouse Rock* ends happily. For the sultry, dark-eyed Judy Tyler, however, there would be no more happy endings. Shortly after the film's release on 21 October 1957, her young and promising life was tragically snuffed out like the flame of candle in the wind. She was killed in an automobile accident near Billy The Kid, Wyoming at the age of 24.

For Elvis too, the mood was becoming more serious. The kid from Memphis had matured. The best-selling novel *A Stone for Danny Fisher*, by Harold Robbins, was being considered for the script of the Paramount picture *King Creole*, a film which was intended to showcase Elvis in his first 'serious' dramatic role. Though it would include 13 songs, such as 'Crawfish,' 'As Long as I Have You,' 'Lover Doll,' 'Hard Headed Woman' and 'Loyal and True,' it is remembered by many critics as Elvis' best film.

As the fall of 1957 gave way to winter and talk of *King Creole* swirled around him like the dried leaves wind-borne over Judy Tyler's grave, another dark cloud loomed out of the east to cast its sinister shadow across the path of the once happy-go-lucky Elvis. Five days before Christmas, the Memphis Draft Board gave the millionaire King of Rock and Roll 30 days to report for duty in the US Army.

Elvis, as Vince Everett, becomes a big star, but success does not cure Vince's egotism, as we can see *above*. **It's only after he goes through travails with Peggy Van Alden (Judy Tyler),** *at top and right,* **and gets beaten up by his buddy, that he softens.**

ELVIS
The GI Years

By 1958 Elvis was at the peak of his career, yet over his head hung the Selective Service. Speculation ran rampant that Elvis would be able to 'pull strings' and somehow get out of his military obligations. Most entertainers who *were* ultimately drafted during the 1950s were assigned to a Special Services unit where they could continue to entertain as well as maintain some kind of contact with the public, so most people believed that this would be Elvis' lot if he did wind up serving as a draftee. And he did serve. Elvis pulled no strings save to request a two-month deferment to finish *King Creole*. On 24 March 1958, Elvis and his parents walked through a gauntlet of reporters to the Memphis induction center.

The following day, Private Presley (serial number US53310761) arrived in Fort Chaffee, Arkansas to have the distinctive sideburns and ducktail of an earlier era shorn away.

As Elvis had pulled no strings to stay *out* of the Army, neither did he opt for Special Services. If he was in the Army, he was in the Army, so the new private requested assignment to the Tank Corps!

Elvis was busy in boot camp when *King Creole*, his fourth film, premiered on 4 June. Two months later, however, he received a special leave to go to the bedside of his sick mother. On 14 August, two days after her son arrived in Memphis, Gladys Presley succumbed to a heart attack complicated by hepatitis at the age of 46.

A month later, Elvis completed basic training at Fort Hood, Texas and on 19 September 1958, Elvis was shipped to Germany as part of Combat Command C of the 3rd Armored Division—the 'Mailed Fist of NATO.' Arriving in Germany on the first of October, he was stationed in the town of Friedburg, about half an hour northeast of Frankfurt. The command barracks had, during World War II, housed Hitler's SS Troops.

The Army made a special point of trying to keep reporters away from him and thus keep his name out of the papers. Even though the country was at peace, Private Presley was assigned to a combat-ready armored division ready to move into the thick of international conflict at a moment's notice. Elvis spent most of his days as a jeep driver in a reconnaissance

On 24 March 1958, Elvis didn't just get inducted, he requested the tank service! Like many others, the King started as a private and worked his way up to sergeant. *At below and at right* is Sergeant Presley on patrol during Winter Shield exercises, in West Germany in 1960. With him are driver Private Lonnie Wolfe and machine gunner Spec 4 Hal Miller.

platoon until being promoted to sergeant in January 1960. Historians may ignore it, but the fact remains that the Soviet Union made no attempt to invade western Europe while Elvis Presley was in the US Army in Germany!

The general belief was that the Army and the middle class establishment were going to put the gyrating wild child Elvis in his place once and for all. Rumor at the time even had it that Colonel Parker, upset at some of Elvis' excesses, had planned the Army hitch in order to clean up the public image of this 'Frank Sinatra' of his generation! It is interesting to note that even though Elvis was subjected to the normal rigors of Army life, he was permitted to live off-post since he could claim one dependent, his recently widowed father, Vernon. Elvis was permitted to move not only his father but his grandmother, Minnie Mae, and two long-time friends, Lenore Fike and Red West, to Germany to be with him.

The clan from Memphis set up housekeeping in the nearby town of Bad Nauheim, where a sign appeared in front of the Presley house at 14 Goethestrasse which read 'Autogramme Von 19:30-20:00-Nur Bitte' ('Autographs from 7:30-8:00 pm only please'). Each evening there would assemble a group of young European fans, many of whom had travelled hundreds of miles for the privilege of being lucky enough to see Elvis in person, even if it was only for a brief moment.

In August 1959, during a visit to the Eagles club, a social club for American service families, Elvis was introduced to Priscilla Beaulieu, the 14-year-old step-daughter of US Air Force Captain Paul Beaulieu. Though he was 10 years her elder, they dated heavily, but their relationship remained technically platonic. The fact that the relationship between Elvis and Priscilla remained above board, was, as she has noted in her

Above: **This photo, taken in Bavaria, illustrates that Elvis participated fully in Army life. Here he is shown examining a trouble spot on his jeep with Private Wolfe. But way before you're a sergeant, you're a private! The photo *below* shows Private Presley during a training exercise in 1959. He was generally an 'OK Joe.'**

This page: Released while he was in the Army, *King Creole* showcased Elvis at his film noir sexiest. *Below,* Elvis as Danny Fisher confronts Walter Matthau, as gang leader Maxie Fields, and Maxie's girfriend, Ronnie—Carolyn Jones, who later played Morticia Adams in TV's *The Adams Family*.

1985 autobiography *Elvis and Me*, a source a great frustration for Priscilla. However, Captain Beaulieu was not impressed by the King of Rock 'n Roll. He demanded—unsuccessfully—that the relationship be brought to an end immediately. The two dated for nearly a year, and in fact a tearful Priscilla accompanied Elvis to Wiesbaden airport on 2 March 1960 when he departed Germany.

While in the Army, Elvis naturally wondered, along with many others, about how he would be received when he returned to civilian life. Many of his detractors loudly proclaimed that his audiences would soon fade away once he was inducted. They were proved wrong. His popularity actually grew in strength due to RCA's releasing of pre-recorded hits like 'Hound Dog,' 'All Shook Up' and 'Now or Never' during his tour of duty.

Elvis now wanted to develop his talents beyond singing. He wanted to be an actor capable of performing in serious non-singing roles. That ambition would lead him to abandon live performances once he returned to civilian life in favor of producing an average of three motion pictures a year. By the mid-60s he would become the highest paid actor in Hollywood.

On 3 March 1960, having left Priscilla Beaulieu in Germany, Elvis stepped off a military air transport at McGuire AFB, New Jersey into the waiting arms of Frank Sinatra's daughter Nancy. Flashbulbs popped and rumors flew. Two days later, he was officially discharged at nearby Fort Dix. The King was again a civilian.

When Elvis left the Army, he was a sergeant earning a little more than seven dollars per paycheck. On 7 March, at 7:40 in the morning, he arrived back home in Memphis aboard a private train to the welcome of a huge and adoring crowd. Even though he was relieved at having survived the Army experience, he was apprehensive about returning to Graceland. The sprawling estate on US Highway 51 on the south side of Memphis had been a gift from him to his mother in March 1957, a year before she died. Nothing could relieve Elvis' grief at having to return home without her there to greet him.

Above: Elvis fields media flak before his discharge from the US Army in March of 1960. *Below:* Sergeant Presley arrives at a press conference at Fort Dix, New Jersey, in the company of Nancy Sinatra. *At right:* He receives his final pay and release from duty on 5 March 1960.

ELVIS The Hollywood Years

Having returned to civilian life, the former Sergeant Presley lost no time in returning to the glitter and glamour of the entertainment world. In his first month out of the Army on 5 March 1960, he completed two recording sessions at RCA's Nashville studios. The tracks included 'Soldier Boy,' 'It Feels So Right,' 'Reconsider Baby,' 'It's Now or Never' and the immortal 'Are You Lonesome Tonight.'

On 26 March, Elvis went south to Miami for *Frank Sinatra's Welcome Home Party for Elvis Presley* which would be aired on ABC television in May, and then jetted to Hollywood to renew his long dormant movie career. Indeed, his recording career would now take a back seat to his film career. Most of the songs that he did record during the 1960s would be for his movies.

Hal Wallis, who had helped launch the careers of Charlton Heston, Burt Lancaster, Shirley MacLaine and Kirk Douglas, now had a new screen *idol* on his hands. Wallis believed from Elvis' first screen test that he could become a star of greater magnitude than Valentino. Time would prove his estimation to be prophetic.

Elvis's first movie after his hitch in the Army was based on his 24 months in the service. In *GI Blues*, still sporting his GI haircut, Elvis played Tulsa McCauley, a young soldier stationed in Frankfurt, Germany. He becomes involved with a beautiful German cabaret performer named Lili (Juliet Prowse) whom he finally wins over despite various layers of difficulty. Among the 10 songs that he recorded for the film are 'Pocketful of Rainbows,' a duet with Juliet Prowse, and a lullaby sung to a baby and a serenade to a marionette in which the King of Rock 'n Roll is backed by a children's chorus. No one could now say that his musical repertoire lacked variety! Other cast members included James Douglas, Robert Ivers, Leticia Ronan and Sigrid Maier.

Even as he was finishing *GI Blues*, Elvis was courting Sandy Ferra, whom he had met on 21 April (see page 6). He

Below is a scene from *Flaming Star*, depicting doomed good times for the Burton family. Co-star Barbara Eden, as Pacer Burton's (Elvis) fiancee, is at photo right. The selection of leading ladies would become immense, and some, such as Ann-Margret *(at right)* turned into serious affairs.

36

was also already beginning work on *Flaming Star*, his second film in half a year. In this, his second western, Elvis played Pacer Burton, part white and part Kiowa Indian, who is torn between two worlds. When war breaks out between the Indians and whites, Elvis and his Kiowa mother (Delores del Rio) find themselves in a conflict that can have no happy ending. The film ends tragically and is a commentary on the futility of prejudice. As such, it was ahead of its time—the 1960s had just begun.

His two films of 1960 were released on 20 October and 20 December respectively—into the waiting arms of a multitude of fans longing to spend the Yuletide with their idol after his two years of absence from the silver screen. For Elvis himself, Christmas 1960 meant leaving behind the palm trees of Southern California for the snow-shrouded grounds of Graceland. He was joined there by his father, his father's new wife Davada 'Dee' Presley and Priscilla Beaulieu. For Priscilla, Christmas 1960 meant a six-week-old 'hound dog' of her very own, and the implied promise that—despite the continuing platonic relationship—the hand of Elvis would one day also be hers. Nevertheless, she rejoined her family for a time.

At left: Pacer Burton (Elvis) and Roslyn Pierce (Barbara Eden) in a still from *Flaming Star*, a tragic film that portrayed the stupidity of prejudice. Elvis wore his old Army khakis in *GI Blues* and *Blue Hawaii* *(above)*—the latter of which grossed $4.7 million.

After Priscilla returned to Germany, Elvis remained in Tennessee for a while before going back to California. It was during this time, on 8 March 1961, that the state legislature in Nashville named him an honorary Tennessee Colonel. It is a little known fact that after that date, the former US Army sergeant was no longer outranked by Colonel Tom Parker!

While in Nashville, Elvis recorded more than two dozen songs which would form the backbone of the soundtracks for *Wild In the Country* and *Blue Hawaii*, his 1961 films. American playwright Clifford Odets created the role of Glen Tyler in *Wild In the Country* especially for Elvis. The concept of the budding young talent is coupled with a confused and rebellious side that creates a character of some depth. Cliff (Gary Lockwood) and Noreen (Tuesday Weld) try to keep Glen on his road to no good while his counselor, Irene (Hope Lange), and childhood sweetheart, Betty Lee (Millie Perkins) struggle with the forces of darkness, trying to build, encourage, understand and open doors of opportunity for the promising novelist. Elvis leaves us at movie's end at a college desk working toward his dream of a writing career. Also in the cast was 1960 Olympic decathlon gold medalist Rafer Johnson, who would later be the man to light the torch for the 1984 Olympics in Los Angeles.

Blue Hawaii was one of the most successful of all Elvis films, grossing $4.7 million in an era when movies cost less than a dollar to see. Elvis portrays the rebellious son of a pineapple tycoon who is trying to make his own way in life amid numerous romantic entanglements. Elvis essentially played himself, and this, probably more than any other factor, contributed to the film's overwhelming success. The film was directed by Norman Taurog and produced for Paramount for Hal Wallis. Hawaii's natural splendors provided a magnificent backdrop for the film and four years later Elvis' second Hawaii-based film, *Paradise, Hawaiian Style* was produced.

Blue Hawaii was released on 14 November 1961. On 18

Above: Glenn Tyler (Elvis) and Noreen (Tuesday Weld) in *Wild in the Country*. Tuesday was one of three female leads playing opposite Elvis—including Hope Lange and Millie Perkins (as Betty Lee, Glenn's faithful childhood sweetheart, *at right*). Elvis portrayed an angry young man, loaded with talent, who is struggling to be a novelist.

January 1962, 10 days after his 27th birthday, Elvis signed a multimillion dollar five-year contract with Hal Wallis. The first film produced under this new contract was the romantic comedy *Follow That Dream*, based on the novel *Pioneer, Go Home*. Elvis played Toby Kwimper, son of a Florida homesteader. He and his family fight the establishment with their down-home ways and beat the system. *Follow That Dream*'s director, Gordon Douglas, is said to have concentrated on Elvis as an actor rather than as a singer, even though the King does sing five songs in the film. *Follow That Dream* was released in April 1962, followed by *Kid Galahad* and *Girls! Girls! Girls!* in August and October. By the release dates, Elvis was already in the studio, recording the soundtrack for films which would be released in 1963.

In *Kid Galahad* (a remake of the 1937 Edward G Robinson-Humphrey Bogart film) Elvis played Walter Gulick, the original Rocky, a country boy who, after becoming a sparring partner at a boxing training camp, fights his way up the long ladder to fame and glory. To get into shape for the film, Elvis trained with ex-world junior welterweight, Mushy Callahan. Charles Bronson, in a preview of his tough guy roles a decade later, played his trainer. Songs in this film included the now-forgotten 'Key to the Whole Wide World,' 'This is Living,' 'Riding the Rainbow,' 'Home Is Where the Heart Is,' 'I Got Lucky' and 'A Whistling Tune.'

In *Girls! Girls! Girls!* Elvis played the part of Ross Carpenter, a fisherman trying to recover a sailboat that had been built by his father, but which had been lost to outsiders due to the family's lack of funds. The director was a veteran Elvis co-worker, Norman Taurog, while the producer was, again, Hal Wallis for Paramount. This film is a light musical romance in which Ross becomes involved in a menage a trois with Robin Gantner (Stella Stevens) and Laurel Dodge (Laurel Goodwin). The songs included the title track as well as one of his more

At left: Elvis as Chad Gates, with one of many belles in *Blue Hawaii*. *Above,* Elvis in a creative moment with his youngest co-star, Vicky Tiu, in *It Happened at the World's Fair*. *At right:* As *Kid Galahad*.

remembered show tunes 'Return to Sender.' The musical score was written and conducted by Joseph J Lelley. The Jordanaires, Elvis' backup group from his pre-Army days, provided vocal accompaniment.

In October Elvis went to Seattle, where the 1962 World's Fair was used as the backdrop for his twelfth movie (his eighth in just over two years). *It Happened at the World's Fair* starred Elvis as a high-flying pilot who becomes romantically involved with Joan O'Brian in the process of repossessing his repossessed airplane. The romance is complicated by seven-year-old Sue-Lin (Vicky Tiu), a Chinese orphan whose uncle has mysteriously disappeared. Elvis takes Sue-Lin under his wing and one of the highlights of the movie is a duet in which Elvis sings with Vicki Tiu 'How Would You Like To Be.' Elvis also sings a duet with Joan entitled 'Happy Ending.' Other tunes included 'Take Me To the Fair,' an oblique reference to the 1904 show tune 'Take Me to St Louis, Louis, Take Me To the Fair.'

Released in April 1963, *World's Fair* was followed by *Fun in Acapulco* (released in November 1963), for which Elvis recorded a series of Spanish-language songs, including 'El Toro,' 'Malaguena,' 'Guadalajara' and three versions of 'Vino, Dinero y Amor' in a 22-23 January 1963 session in Hollywood. In *Fun in Acapulco*, Elvis co-stars with Alejandro Rey as a trapeze artist who has a close call with death and is thereafter afraid of heights. He takes a job as a lifeguard at an Acapulco hotel near the famous cliff-diving locale. Naturally, romance is involved, this time with two beautiful women, Ursula Andress and Elsa Cardenas. By the end of the film, Elvis has overcome his fears and won the heart of Ursula.

Released on 6 March 1964, MGM's *Kissin' Cousins* was a unique motion picture. Elvis actually played a dual role in which he returned to olive drab as Lieutenant Josh Morgan, a

Kissin' Cousins: Two Elvises in one film! *At left* is Elvis as Josh Morgan, shown here with Azalea Tatum (Yvonne Craig), and *above* as Jodie Tatum, whose love interest (not shown) is Midge, a WAC (Cynthia Pepper). *Overleaf:* High times for the Tatum clan in *Kissin' Cousins*.

young Army officer assigned to run a Tennessee hillbilly family off of their land so the government can build a missile base there. He *also* played Jodie Tatum, a member of that family. In a film whose symbolism has been heatedly discussed in psychology classes for years, Elvis the 'Hillbilly Cat' fights Elvis the Army officer. Split-image techniques allow both Elvises to appear on the screen simultaneously! Lance LeGault also played the *back of Elvis* in a wig!

Ultimately, Josh Morgan discovers that he is a distant cousin to the identical, albeit lighter-haired Tatum, and to sisters Selena and Azelea Tatum (Pam Austin and Yvonne Craig), whom—you guessed it—he kisses!

Released a little more than a month after *Kissin' Cousins*, *Viva Las Vegas* found Elvis paired with a red-hot Ann-Margret as his leading lady. Elvis is an aspiring race driver and Ann-Margret plays a swimming instructor. Ann-Margret sings 'My Rival' and joins Elvis for the duet 'The Lady Loves Me.' The race car sequences directed by George Sidney feature plenty of action but, of course the teaming of Elvis and Ann-Margret provided the movie with a high-octane raciness.

Movie magic: *Two Elvises* occupy the center of the set *at right* with Cynthia Pepper, on the left, and Yvonne Craig in the big hoedown scene in *Kissin' Cousins*. **Above:** A poster for the film.

48

The torrid love affair between Elvis and Ann-Margret started late in 1963 during the filming of *Viva Las Vegas*, lasted for months, and caused a serious rift between Elvis and Priscilla. Shown *on these pages* are stills of Elvis and Ann-Margret from the motion picture.

Elvis returned to Hawaii for *Paradise Hawaiian Style* with Suzanne Leigh, big production numbers and stunning Hawaiian scenery.

52

A cast of award-winning stars including Barbara Stanwyck and Jack Albertson combined to make *Roustabout* (released in November 1964) another Elvis film that fans simply could not miss. Stanwyck plays the owner of a carnival who discovers Charlie Rogers' (Elvis) singing ability and provides a stage for him to perform such songs as 'One Track Mind,' 'I Never Had It So Good' and 'Hard Knocks.' This Hal Wallis production offered Elvis the 'hard guy but soft touch' role that he had come to establish as a formula.

Between 1965 and 1968, Rock 'n Roll came of age and fomented the most far-reaching revolution in the entire history of popular music. During these same years, Elvis Presley—the man who had sparked this revolution with his 1954–1957 recordings and who had inspired an entire generation of musicians—sat by in Hollywood, ignoring the music scene. While the musical genre that he practically invented evolved into one of the century's most important art forms, Elvis was making what are regarded as his worst films. Nothing from this period had the power of *Jailhouse Rock*, the intensity of *King Creole*, the raw excitement of *Wild in the Country* nor the depth of *Kid Galahad*. Indeed, and alas, next to the Beatles' *A Hard Days Night* (1964) and *Help!* (1965), the scripts that Elvis was forced to endure during the mid-sixties read like soap operas.

Yet he made them. Three a year. Year after year. In *Girl Happy* (1965), Rusty (Elvis) was hired to protect Valerie (Shelley Fabares)—the daughter of a Chicago nightclub owner—from Ft Lauderdale, Florida's beachbums. Rusty and Valerie find themselves involved in mass arrests, barroom brawls and pool-side song and dance that never ends. Songs include 'She's Evil,' 'Do the Clam,' and 'Puppet on a String.' Elvis captivates the beach crowd in the movie just as he did the movie's adoring audiences.

Tickle Me (1965) stars Elvis as Lonnie Beal, a radio writer who takes a job at a beauty spa-dude ranch. Elvis romances a British actress, Jocelyn Lane, while singing nine songs including 'It's a Long Lonely Highway,' 'It Feels So Right' and 'Dirty, Dirty Feeling.' The cast included Julie Adams, Jack Mullaney, Mary Anders, Edward Faulkner and Bill Williams.

As usual, southern California was the location, although an ersatz Middle East was the background, for the movie *Harum Scarum* (1965). Elvis plays a star who has travelled to the land of the Arabian Nights for the premier of his latest motion picture. Fantasy and fun lead Elvis into adventure as he is kidnapped, drawn into murderous plots, and finally worked up as a Rudolph Valentino-style hero who wins the hand of Princess Shalimar (Mary Ann Mobley). Songs include 'Harem Holiday' and 'Go East, Young Man,' and once again the Jordanaires provide accompaniment for the music. Gerald Drayson Adams' screen play and Gene Nelson's direction compliment each other well. Fran Jeffries, Michael Ansara and Jay Novello complete the list of leading cast members.

'Frankie and Johnny Were Lovers' is a phrase familiar to all sing-along fans. In the ballad-inspired movie *Frankie and Johnny* (1966), the lovers were Elvis (Johnny), as a compulsive gambler, and Donna Douglas (Frankie). In the film, Frankie found herself fighting thoughts of murder when Johnny turned to Nancy Kovack to bring him luck at the tables. With choreography by Earl Burton, Elvis is seen in

At left: Elvis and Nellie Bly (Nancy Kovack), with Harry Morgan in *Frankie and Johnny*. Harry Morgan, once Jack Webb's sidekick on *Dragnet*, later starred in the TV version of *M*A*S*H*.

what was his first dancing role since *Jailhouse Rock* (1957) and still manages to sing his way through the film with such songs as 'Come Along,' 'Look Out,' 'Broadway,' 'Shout It Out' and 'Beginner's Luck,' not to mention the title song and the ever-favorite 'When the Saints Come Marching In.' Cast members included Sue Ane Langdon, Anthony Eisley, Robert Strauss, Audrey Christie and Harry Morgan. *Paradise-Hawaiian Style* (1966) seemed a natural follow-up to the success of *Blue Hawaii*, filmed four years earlier. Elvis and James Shegeta play helicopter pilot tour guides who show 'Hawaii at its best' to vacationers. Elvis sings alone and in duets such tunes as 'You Scratch My Back,' 'House of Sand' and 'Datin'.' Seventy Hawaiian musicians joined him for the movie's big production number. In *Spinout* (1966) Elvis combines the role of race driver that he played in *Viva Las Vegas* (1964) with the role of singer he'd played both in several movies and in his real life. Literally, every girl in this picture is in love with Elvis. Elvis sings nine songs including 'Smorgasbord,' and 'I'll Be Back.' The cast included Shelley Fabares, Sandy Ferra, Diane McBain, Deborah Walley, Dodie Marshall, Jack Mullaney, Will Hutchins, Warren Berlinger, Jimmy Hawkins and Carl Betz.

Easy Come, Easy Go (1967) put Elvis back into uniform in the role of Ted Jackson, a US Navy demolitions man who is on mine-disposal duties off the coast of California. He meets Jo Symington (Dodie Marshall) who puts him on to the existence of treasure believed to be upon a sunken ship once owned by her grandfather. As might have been suspected, Elvis finds the treasure and ultimately Jo's heart. Most critics liked *Easy Come, Easy Go* probably because of the Allan Weiss/Anthony Lawrence script and the directing of John Rich. Songs in the film included 'Easy Come, Easy Go' and 'Yoga Is As Yoga Does.' The cast also included Pat Priest, Pat Harrington, Skip Ward and Elsa Lanchester—who had created the title role in the original *Bride of Frankenstein* and, in this case, the crazy yogi Madame Neherina opposite Elvis Presley's Ted Jackson.

Filmed with a British setting at the same time that the Beatles were recording *Sgt Pepper's Lonely Hearts Club Band* in the EMI Abbey Road studios in London, *Double Trouble* (1967) underscored how far the fantasy world created for Elvis in Hollywood had drifted from the leading edge of the musical genre that the King had helped create. In this strangely timeless adventure film, Elvis plays Guy Lambert, a singer who roams around Europe, being pursued for kidnapping as well as diamond theft. Elvis sings nine songs including the title song and 'City by Night,' 'I Love Only One Girl,' 'Could I Fall in Love,' and 'There's So Much World to See.' Elvis and his leading lady Annette Day literally sail off into the sunset at the film's ending. The cast included John Williams, Yvonne Roman, the Wiere Brothers, Chips Rafferty and Norman Rossington. In *Clambake* (1967) Elvis is cast as Scott Heyward, a multi-millionaire's son who exchanged identities with Will Hutchins, a water ski instructor. Director Arthur Nadel actually used film footage from the Orange Bowl International Power Boat Regatta. Romance and jealousy ensue, but the film ultimately ends happily. The movie's musical numbers included the title song as well as 'The House That Has Everything,' 'Confidence,' 'You Don't Know Me,' 'The Girl I Never Knew' and 'Who Needs Money.' The cast also included Shelley Fabares, Bill Bixby and Gary Merrill.

Stay Away, Joe (1968) shows Elvis in a wild west setting as Navajo Indian Joe Lightcloud, whose parents (Burgess

Multi-millionaire's son Scott Heyward, in *Clambake (above)*, and pilot Mike Edwards *(facing page)*, in *It Happened at the World's Fair*, were typical of the types of roles Elvis played in the 1960s.

Elvis and Annette Day are seen *above*, as Guy Lambert and Jill Conway, in *Double Trouble*. Guy is on the lam in Europe. Though all is fine by movie's end, it's trouble, trouble *(overleaf)* until then.

Meredith and Katie Jurado) are Arizona cattle ranchers. The days are filled with roping and branding followed by nights of drinking and brawling. Elvis is a cow poke, naturally irresistible to all the local women. In one humorous scene, Elvis even sings to Dominic, a bull on the ranch. The songs included 'Stay Away, Mame' and 'All I Needed was the Rain.'

Later in the year Elvis was cast alongside 1930s singing star Rudy Vallee in *Live A Little, Love A Little* (1968), a romantic comedy based on Dan Greenberg's novel *Kiss My Firm but Pliant Lips*. Vallee played an advertising executive who hired Elvis in his role as a fashion photographer with a complicated and intertwined personal and professional life. Elvis sang four songs including 'Almost in Love' and 'A Little Less Conversation' but missed a fabulous opportunity for a duet with Vallee. The cast also included Michelle Carey, Don Porter, Brooke Sargent, Sterling Holloway and Celeste Yarnall.

If the opportunity for a duet with Rudy Vallee was allowed to slip away forever, a similar occasion was in fact captured a few months later when Elvis was cast opposite Nancy Sinatra in *Speedway* (1968), his third role as a race car driver. An IRS agent seems an unlikely player in an Elvis Presley movie, and perhaps no one short of Nancy Sinatra could have slipped such a role into the Elvis style. Together they sing their way

Elvis wore a variety of movie getups—one of the more unusual of which is seen *above*. *At right* is Elvis as Steve Grayson, in *Speedway*; his co-star was Nancy Sinatra, as IRS investigator Susan Jacks.

59

Above: One of Elvis' endless stock of vulnerable expressions. **At right:** Even as Michelle Carey bedded the King down on the tastefully decorated set of *Live a Little, Love a Little* (1968), his thoughts seemed miles away. Live performance was again in the offing.

into and out of plots, places and romance. Elvis sings the title song along with 'Let Yourself Go,' 'Your Time Hasn't Come Yet,' 'Baby' and 'He's Your Uncle, Not Your Dad,' while Ms Sinatra solos on 'Your Groovy Self' and both join in 'There Ain't Nothing Like a Song.' Other *Speedway* cast members include Bill Bixby, William Schallert, Victoria Meyerink, Ross Hagen and Gale Gordon—whose career credits have included starring roles opposite Eve Arden in *Our Miss Brooks*, and opposite Lucille Ball in her post-Desi Arnez sitcom.

After an unbroken string of nearly 20 musical comedies, *Charro* (1969) was a period western, conceived as a showcase for Elvis in his first dramatic film since *Kid Galahad* (1962). It was a serious role for a maturing actor in changing times. Critics who had ignored his happy-go-lucky films of the mid-1960s were compelled to take a serious look at *Charro*. Unfortunately, the reviews were mixed, and sadly, the film would be Elvis' last role of this type. In *Charro*, Elvis plays a reformed outlaw who saves a Western town from his former gang's control. The title song—the only song—was written by Hugo Montenegro with lyrics by Alan and Marilyn Bergman. The cast included Ina Balin, Victor French, Lynn Kellogg, Barbara Werle and Solomon Sturges.

In *The Trouble With Girls* (1969), Elvis plays Walter Hale, the manager of a chautauqua company of actors and enter-

61

tainers touring the Midwest during the 1920s. Elvis sings the beautiful spiritual, 'Swing Low Sweet Chariot,' as well as 'Signs of the Zodiac' and 'Almost.' The cast included Marilyn Mason, Nicole Jaffe, Sheree North, Edward Andrew, John Carradine, Anissa Jones, Vincent Price and Joyce Van Paten.

The last film that Elvis would make in Hollywood was *Change of Habit* (1970), in which he was cast as Dr John Carpenter, head of a clinic in a Puerto Rican neighborhood. *Change of Habit* was actually a sort of hybrid in which Elvis was cast in a dramatic non-singing role in a sitcom style film in the mold of his two dozen musical comedies of the preceding decade. The sitcom nature of *Change of Habit* was underscored by the presence of Mary Tyler Moore, late of the *Dick Van Dyke Show*, who would soon become a household word with a hit series of her own. As the plot unfolds, Dr Carpenter is assigned three young female assistants, without being told that they are in fact a trio of Catholic nuns. He falls in love with Sister Michelle (Mary Tyler Moore) who returns his love in spite of herself. The conflicts are momentous and she must decide whether to leave Elvis or her church. The movie ends as a cliffhanger because neither the audience nor Elvis knows what her decision is going to be. Indeed, 'cliffhanger' was then an allegory for Elvis' own movie career as his fans were left to wonder whether he would ever make another film. Though he was to make no further films other than documentaries, he did pass up what would have been a spectacular venue for his talents that could well have earned him an academy award nomination. In August 1974, he turned down an invitation to appear with Barbra Streisand in a remake of *A Star is Born* because he would have had to share top billing.

Many critics have maligned Elvis' decade in Hollywood by saying that he wasted his enormous talents in a series of films that were either shallow or shoddy. While it is true that he never earned an Oscar nomination (some say he never came even close), it is equally true that each one of his 31 pictures made money! That fact speaks for itself.

In 14 years in Hollywood, Elvis' image changed from the cocky innocence of the Hillbilly Cat *(above)* **to the mature actor straining to bring life to the serious role of Jess Wade in** *Charro* **(at right).**

ELVIS
His Private Life

In the films that Elvis Presley made between 1960 and 1970, he played a wide variety of genre roles ranging from race car drivers to sailors and from circus performers to cowboys. One thing, however, that these roles had in common was that they represented the types of careers that might have been aspired to by a kid graduating from high school in Memphis in the mid-1950s. They were all jobs in which Elvis Aron Presley might ultimately have ended up had he not first become the King of Rock 'n Roll.

But he *had* become the King, and no matter how deeply he was submerged into the fantasy life of his Hollywood alter egos, there was no escaping one critical fact: He was not the happy-go-lucky young buck in the movies, he was Elvis Presley. And therein lay the enigma: who, in fact, was Elvis Presley?

There were three Elvis Presleys: First, there was the King of Rock 'n Roll, who had emerged between 1954 and 1958, and who had given a few concert performances in 1960 and 1961. The King was known primarily for his early recordings, which now shed their vital influence across the length and breadth of rock 'n roll in the 1960s. They did so alone, because the man himself had vanished.

Second, there was the Elvis Presley of Hollywood who was known to millions upon millions through his three films a

Behind the walls of fortress Graceland *(above)*—the myriad achievements of a lifetime *(facing page)* and the accoutrements of a reclusive lifestyle *(below)*. Graceland was home and refuge.

year, year after year. This was the Elvis who was *every* man and yet was so elusive as to be *no* man beyond a fleeting flicker of light that smiled upon the silver screen—and then blurred into a succession of almost identical incarnations.

Finally, there was Elvis Aron Presley, a human being whose life had changed so quickly and so dramatically that he hardly knew himself. Indeed, he was a private person that hardly anyone would know, a man who was as different from Ross Carpenter in *Girls! Girls! Girls!* or Mike McCoy in *Spinout* as night is different from day.

How could the fans who went to theaters on Christmas 1967 to see Scott Heyward race his boat across Biscayne Bay in *Clambake* have known that Elvis Presley hated the script, and felt compelled to make it because his father convinced him they needed the money to pay their taxes?

So much about the private life of Elvis Presley remains shrouded in mystery and innuendo, that it has given rise to a catalog of apocryphal tales which still continues to expand. Yet, truth is often stranger than fiction, and there are few important elements of Elvis' enigmatic life that are stranger than his relationship with Priscilla Ann Beaulieu.

He had met and dated the beautiful teenager when he was in the Army in Germany in 1959, and had maintained an intermittent long-distance relationship with her during his first years back in civilian life. Gradually the mutual attraction became an obsession and Elvis insisted that Priscilla move back to the United States to be near him. This request was obviously complicated by the fact that she was an average high school student and he was not only a man in his late 20s, but a film and recording star of immense proportions. In her autobiography, Priscilla cites this dichotomy as being particularly hard on her step-father. On one hand, most fathers would not mind having a daughter courted by a millionaire, but when that daughter is only 16 years old, and the millionaire is 10 years older and is a man with the reputation that Elvis had in the early 1960s, the alarm bells will certainly start to ring.

Add to this Elvis' insistence that Priscilla leave home to come to Memphis, and you have the portrait of an extraordinarily distraught Captain Paul Beaulieu. To assuage his fears, Elvis told the captain that he would arrange for Priscilla to live, not at Graceland, but with Vernon Presley and his new wife Dee.

At last Priscilla won her mother over to her cause and finally, in 1962, Paul Beaulieu relented. Two first class airline tickets arrived courtesy of Elvis, and Mr Beaulieu and his daughter set out for Hollywood—where filming for *Fun in Acapulco* was underway—to discuss the arrangement.

Having won over her father with his well-known charm, Elvis sent Priscilla to Memphis where she moved in with Vernon and Dee, and was enrolled in the Immaculate Conception High School, a Catholic girls' school.

Ironically, Priscilla was now alone, because Elvis remained in Hollywood to finish the film. When Elvis at last returned to Graceland, Priscilla's life finally changed, although not nearly in the way that might have been suspected.

In Greek mythology there is the story of Pygmalion, the King of Cyprus who carved, and then fell in love with, a statue

Above: Elvis Presley's gold-plated '59 Cadillac is now in the Country Music Hall of Fame in Nashville; even the paint had 24-karat flecks in it! Elvis and Priscilla would go for long midnight drives in this car.

At right: The King and his Colonel. Except for his most private moments within the grounds of Graceland, Colonel Tom Parker managed Elvis' life until 22 January 1976, when they parted ways.

of a beautiful woman—who only at the end of the story is brought to life. In her autobiography, Priscilla likens Elvis' relationship with her to that of Pygmalion and his beautiful Galatea. Indeed, Elvis had told Priscilla that one day they would marry, but he became obsessed with the notion that she would be a virgin bride.

Nevertheless, Elvis secretly moved Priscilla into Graceland well before her graduation from high school. At Graceland, he bought her wardrobes upon wardrobes full of clothes and took a minutely detailed interest in her appearance and style of dress. They would both, in fact, dress for dinner even though they were dining at home!

On 10 June 1963, when Priscilla graduated from high school, Elvis was waiting outside in a limousine to whisk her back to fortress Graceland—from which neither of them would emerge for days, and sometimes weeks, at a time.

For the next four years, their life was a constant cycle of seclusion alternated with Elvis' absences to make his thrice-yearly movies. Elvis continued in his firm conviction that Priscilla would remain a virgin until they married, but at the same time he would not give any indication of *when* he intended to wed her.

For Priscilla this frustration alternated with her loneliness as he made seasonal migrations to Hollywood, and was compounded by the rumors of his romantic involvement with his various co-stars. In her autobiography, Priscilla cites in particular his affair with Ann-Margret during the filming of *Viva Las Vegas* in 1964. In fact, when Priscilla went to Los Angeles with Elvis later in the year, to begin work on *Kissin' Cousins*, the Ann-Margret rumors still persisted and Priscilla returned to Memphis in a huff. Despite her anger, Priscilla realized that he could easily toss her aside, so she reconciled herself to his other life.

Eventually, Priscilla also began to divide her time between Graceland and Elvis' southern California home at 565 Perugia Way, in the exclusive Los Angeles suburb of Bel Air.

It was just before Christmas in 1966, when Elvis, now almost 32 years old, decided to marry Priscilla. After five years of playing Pygmalion, the King would take a wife. He gave her a 3.5 carat diamond ring to mark the occasion, and in February 1967, he bought a 160-acre ranch near Horn Lake, Mississippi as a honeymoon cottage.

The actual wedding took place on 1 May 1967 in Las Vegas. Elvis and Priscilla flew in from Palm Springs, bought a marriage license, and were married at 9:41 am by David Zenoff, a justice of the Nevada state Supreme Court. The formal ceremony and reception—choreographed by Colonel Parker—followed at the Aladdin Hotel. The newlyweds then returned to Palm Springs aboard Frank Sinatra's private jet, to finally consummate their strange four years of cohabitation.

The lavish interior *(above)* of Elvis Presley's gold plated Cadillac featured TV, stereo and a wet bar. He and Priscilla were wed on 1 May 1967, and Elvis bought a 160 acre ranch for their honeymoon cottage. *At right,* the happy couple stands beside their huge wedding cake during the reception at the Aladdin Hotel in Las Vegas, Nevada. Then they were whisked away in Frank Sinatra's private jet.

Lisa Marie Presley, the one and only child of Elvis and Priscilla, was born exactly nine months later, on 1 February 1968 at Baptist Memorial Hospital.

The new child was a joy to both her parents, but the long-awaited married life evolved into a relationship that was far from being the definition of wedded bliss. Soon, not only Elvis, but Priscilla as well, began seeing other people. By 1970, their marriage was what Priscilla would later characterize as 'part time.'

It was at about this time that Elvis' long-dormant singing career begain its renaissance. He spent most of his time either on the road or holding court at his palatial suite in Las Vegas, where he appeared for month-long engagements. Lisa Marie and her mother would visit the King in Las Vegas for birthdays and piles of gifts, but generally the family had little or nothing in the way of family life. In 1971, Elvis bought a Convair 880 and christened it *Lisa Marie*, but its ability to bring its namesake closer to his side was a fleeting and transitory thing.

Finally, in February 1972, Priscilla left Graceland for the last time, taking Lisa with her, and on 18 August, after five years of marriage, Elvis filed for divorce. It was a year later, on 9 October 1973, that the divorce became final. In the settlement, Priscilla received three quarters of a million dollars in cash, an annual payment of $72,000 for ten years, $4200 a month in alimony, $4000 in child support and attorney's fees of $75,000.

Four days later, the King was admitted to Baptist Memorial Hospital in Memphis for hypertension.

On 1 February 1968, Lisa Marie, the daughter of Elvis Presley, was born. Proud papa Elvis named his private jet *(above)* for her. *At right* are Elvis, Priscilla and Lisa Marie Presley, shortly after the birth.

ELVIS
Las Vegas to Graceland

For most of the decade of the 60s, Elvis' career had kept him tied close to Hollywood. His popularity as a recording star continued through much of this time, but began to be diminished somewhat by the changing social and musical tenor of the times, and eventually his record sales began to slow dramatically from the frenetic pace of the 50s.

By 1965, the Beatles, the Rolling Stones and Bob Dylan were fomenting a revolution that was vast in dimension. The musical geography had changed significantly and the political landscape was in upheaval. Elvis, however, seemed to be locked into a bygone world. His personal appearances had come to a standstill in 1961 and as his movie career also began to wind down at the end of the decade, Elvis adopted a reclusive posture in a self-conscious defense of his personal conservative values—which now seemed to fit less and less into a rapidly changing world. The 'Revolution' that the Beatles sang about was on, and it held no room for what the entertainment world classified as 'has beens.' However, as the waves of revolution began somewhat to subside, there quietly arose the unmistakable realization by the people of the 1960s that the personalities now in the forefront of musical culture owed a great debt to the man in Memphis.

John Lennon was reported to have said 'I basically became a musician because of Elvis Presley.' 'Before Elvis there was nothing,' observed Paul McCartney. Even Bob Dylan admitted 'Elvis recorded a song of mine and that's the one recording I treasure most.' Later Bruce Springsteen would say, 'He wrote the book.' At last the world was beginning to realize that Elvis was no minor earth tremor of quick duration, but rather the epicenter itself of an earthquake whose magnitude had literally changed history.

On the surface at least, Elvis had been fabulously successful. His home at Graceland was, and continues to be, a study of his genius. Elvis owned a fleet of Cadillacs as well as other motor vehicles, and even purchased a four engined Convair

Below: The King returned to the stage in 1968 in televised specials, but it wasn't long before he was playing sellout crowds at live concerts. The next time Elvis said 'Viva Las Vegas!' it would not be as in the 1964 movie *(right)*. The image had changed, but the magic was still there!

'When I hear music, I gotta move.' *These pages:* This was his 1968 comeback TV special, taped between 27 and 29 June and aired on 3 December (see text). Elvis turned out a new hit, 'If I Can Dream.'

880 as a private jet. His trophy room was packed with unique memorabilia—including guitars, honorary degrees and motorcycles and many, many other reminders of a full, successful life. Elvis took a direct hand in refurbishing the estate when he bought it—by applying himself to interior decorating. Very fond of television, Elvis designed his recreation room to feature numerous sets by the use of which he could stay in touch simultaneously with many parts of the world.

Elvis also had an interesting personal motto: 'Taking care of business—in a flash!' This logo was abbreviated TCB and is still emblazoned all around the grounds at Graceland.

Elvis was a far more articulate and reflective person than the public ever realized. He never lost touch with the deep spiritual roots he had grown up with. He was a Bible reader and would sometimes launch into lengthy discourses on the Scriptures and their interpretation into everyday life. He enjoyed the works of Kahlil Gibran as well as Hermann Hesse and Joseph Benner. He was also fascinated with, and at at times preoccupied by, the unavoidable finality of death. Stories abound of his taking family members and friends to the Memphis morgue late at night to view embalmed bodies. Some writers have made these midnight forays into ghoulish and ghostly adventures, but they seem to have been more of an attempt at a spiritual awakening to the realization that the pleasures of this life are fleeting at best and totally void of importance at their worst. Above all, there seemed to be a longing on Elvis' part to come to grips with the basic question of life: 'Where did I come from? Why am I here? Where am I going?'

Elvis had not appeared on television (except in telecasts of his Hollywood movies) since his special with Frank Sinatra in 1960, and he had not performed for a live audience since 1961. His five year MGM contract ended in 1968, and he had the long awaited opportunity to move his career into new and challenging dimensions. NBC made him an offer to do his own television special. As fortune would have it, Elvis got along well with the young director, Steve Binder, who because of his youthfulness gave Elvis the opportunity to be creative—to be himself. For two months Elvis worked on preparations for the special. He is said to have worked harder than he had worked on all his movies combined. He began following a diet to control his weight, and both his confidence and his excitement blossomed. Taped between 27 and 29 June 1968, the four-hour session took the form of private concert, with the King, clad in black, singing to a small studio audience. When it aired on 3 December, the tightly-edited 50-minute final cut was the highest-rated special of the year and produced his first million-selling record in years—'If I Can Dream,' which was the finale. It is interesting to note that over half of the songs he selected for the special—such as 'Blue Moon of Kentucky,' 'Heartbreak Hotel,' 'Don't Be Cruel,' 'Hound Dog' and 'Are You Lonesome Tonight'—dated from his 1954–1957 period. 'Jailhouse Rock' was the *only* film song that he chose.

In January and February 1969, just after the special aired, Elvis went into recording session in Memphis. He was on a creative roll, and recorded so many songs during this time that it took RCA over a year to release them all. They included hits like 'In the Ghetto,' 'Kentucky Rain' and 'Suspicious Minds.' Elvis was soon back on the charts again with *new* songs.

Naturally, Elvis wanted to hit the road again and be in contact with live audiences. Colonel Parker cut a near million-dollar deal with the newly completed Las Vegas International

Hotel for Elvis to perform there for a month. The 'has-been' was now, in fact, a 'yet-to-be'—the second coming of Elvis Presley had begun. Elvis recalled, however, that Las Vegas was the only city where he had bombed 13 years earlier, in 1956—and so was going to take no chances this time. The best musicians, sound, lighting technicians, costumers and choreographers available were assembled for the schedule of two shows a night for 28 straight days. Pre-opening publicity was raised to a fever pitch by Colonel Parker. Opening night, 29 July 1969, was by invitation only and it was the hottest dance card Vegas had ever known. The next day, fans of normal strata who held these white-hot tickets streamed to stand at the throne of the King. The women who had screamed for him in person back in the late 50s returned in droves often accompanied by *their* teenage daughters. Although it had been nine years since Elvis had given a live performance, one would not have known it. The audience cheered for the entire two hours. Elvis gyrated his way through 'All Shook Up,' 'Blue Suede Shoes,' 'In the Ghetto,' 'Tiger Man' and 'Can't Help Falling in Love,' alternately pushing and pulling his audience by first coming with old, and then new, material and by interspersing hard rock with lovely romantic ballads.

Since Elvis had excluded her from rehearsals, it was the first time Priscilla had ever seen him perform live and she was astonished. When he finally left the stage everyone was begging for more. In the ensuing weeks Elvis played to a packed house every night, and thousands were turned away. He recorded a live album and returned to the International Hotel again in 26 January 1970, for another million-dollar month. Between 26 February and 1 March, he earned over a million dollars in three nights for six shows in the Houston Astrodome. He electrified his audiences into hysteria. After Houston he played yet another month at the International in August.

After the Las Vegas victory Elvis took his show on the road. Touring was mainly one night stands in stints of three weeks, with two days off and two shows on Saturdays and Sundays. He played 14 cities between 9 September and 17 November 1970, before going back to Las Vegas on 26 January 1971 for another month at the International Hotel. During the spring, he was back in the RCA Nashville studio for another voluminous recording session.

Between 20 July and 6 September he was on stage almost every day, in a gruelling series of shows at the Sahara Tahoe and the International Hotel. As he had in 1970, Elvis spent a month on the road in 1971 playing to fans in twelve cities.

When he returned again to Las Vegas on 26 January 1972, the venue was the Hilton, but again the fans had him back on the Vegas throne. There is something about this city that suited the King. It is a cross between a mirage and an oasis shimmering in the Nevada desert. It is a place where the nights are illuminated as brightly as the days and the distinction between the two is blurred and indistinct. In Vegas the King was at home.

In 1972, though, he made three tours—15 cities in April, eight cities in June and seven cities in November. Elvis had developed an ongoing love affair with his audiences, and they with him. It was almost like the old days of the 1950s. The King was back.

His four days during June 1972, at Madison Square Garden in New York, set an all-time attendance record and grossed $730,000. A film of his concert performances, *Elvis On Tour*, won the Golden Globe Award for best documentary of 1972. On 14 January 1973, his *Aloha from Hawaii* show in

These pages: **Early in 1973, Elvis returned to Hawaii to telecast his *Aloha From Hawaii* show to 500 million fans around the world.**

77

But why was he wearing dark sunglasses and what are all those wallets doing on the desk? *At left and above:* **Elvis' concern about drug abuse led to this famous audience with President Richard Nixon.**

Honolulu was simulcast via satellite to half a billion people in 40 countries.

As the years of touring wore on, a kind of antipathy began to mount. Elvis received a number of death threats which he took perhaps too seriously. He took up karate and earned an eighth degree black belt, believing that assassins 'gloried' in their deeds. He instructed his body guards that any would-be assassin who made an attempt on his life should be 'taken care of' before the police arrived. During this time, Elvis became increasingly concerned about the drug dependence he saw among his coworkers in the entertainment field. His own chemical dependency was increasing due to the almost frenetic pace of his performance schedule, but this in no way abated his concern for others. He was convinced that he would get through to others to kick their habits, and felt that if he were a Federal Narcotics Agent he could do much to reach the youth and get them off of drugs. He hastily wrote President Nixon an impassioned letter explaining his desires, and even managed an audience with Nixon himself in the Oval Office. Elvis not only came away from that meeting wearing a Federal Narcotics Badge, but also with traditional cufflinks presented to him by the President.

Elvis' love for people was legendary—even toward total strangers. The story is told that at one time his attention was called to a story in a Memphis newspaper about an old black woman who needed a new wheelchair. Elvis not only provided the motorized wheelchair, but delivered it himself. He literally picked her up and placed her in it as her Christmas present.

Marital difficulties with Priscilla had been growing for a number of years. Their estrangement with one another had grown into outright separation and on 9 October 1973, the marriage was legally dissolved. Their main concern was their daughter Lisa Marie, and although their individual attorneys had attempted to work out details of custody over a period of months, it was Elvis and Priscilla themselves who eventually resolved them. It was a divorce devoid of the bitter acrimony which usually accompanies such things. They decided that Lisa's custody would be mutually shared by both of them. Elvis and Priscilla even maintained a respectable friendship in the few years remaining of Elvis' life and, in fact, he never bothered to pick up his copies of the final divorce papers.

With his movie career over, Elvis had naturally focused on Vegas appearances and one-night-stand touring, yet had never lost his ambition to be a serious actor. At one time he had even thought of producing and directing motion pictures, but the opportunities just never materialized. When the offer came in 1974 to play the dramatic role of Norman Wayne opposite Barbra Streisand in the Jon Peters remake of *A Star is Born*, Elvis was naturally enthusiastic, but the project ran into a number of difficulties. Jon Peters was an inexperienced director and Elvis would have to take second billing behind Barbra. In Colonel Parker's estimation, this was not in Elvis' best interest, and the project was dropped much to Elvis' disappointment.

By 1973, exhaustion was taking its toll. He missed a couple of dates at the Las Vegas Hilton in February, and his month at the Sahara Tahoe in May had to be cut back by two weeks. In 1974, he did three weeks at the Hilton but only one show a night. In 1975 he made three short appearances at the Hilton and in 1976 he played only a few shows during the first two weeks of December. These were his last appearances on the Las Vegas stage.

Meanwhile, however, his number of one-night stands was increasing dramatically. From 16 cities in 1973, his tour schedule jumped to 45 and 31 in 1974 and 1975, and to an incredible 74 cities between 17 March and New Year's Eve in 1976!

After all those years of seclusion at fortress Graceland, the fans finally had the King back, but the pendulum had swung radically to the other extreme.

Between January 1975 and April 1977, he was hospitalized at Baptist Memorial Hospital several times for maladies ranging from hypertension and impacted colon, to gastroenteritis and a strained back.

Considering the pain he suffered in his final years, it is easy to admire his capacity for love and generosity. It was said by many that once Elvis touched your life, you were never the same. Sometimes Elvis cared for animals as much as he cared for people. Linda Thompson, his long time girlfriend, relates the story of how, when her dog got sick, Elvis leased a Lear Jet and flew her and the dog to a clinic in Boston that specialized in the disease that the dog had been diagnosed as having. The dog died, but for some time after that Elvis would cry when he thought back on the incident. Linda believed that Elvis was hurt so many times by people that he loved that he became a recluse to protect his sensitivities.

Elvis was also capable of great forgiveness. When the book *Elvis: What Happened?* was written by his former bodyguards, Red and Sonny West, it hurt him deeply, but he told Red West that if ever he or his family ever needed anything, he would see that it was provided for them.

Elvis also had his bouts with temper tantrums, being quite as capable of deep rancor as he was of deep love. All those around him could do during such times was to sit through his tirades and keep quiet knowing that when it was eventually over, he would say something like, 'Please don't take it seriously when I blow.' Then he would usually make it up in some way to any he had offended.

Linda Thompson first met Elvis at the Memphian motion

Above and below: **Elvis! The photo *at right* was taken during his 20 minute press conference in New York City on 9 June 1972. Over the next three nights, he played to 80,000 fans at Madison Square Garden, where he cut a live album and grossed $730,000.**

picture theatre on 5 July 1972, at one of Elvis' private screenings. She was then the reigning Miss Tennessee. They were constant companions for half a decade, and did talk a number of times about marriage, but the circumstances just never seemed to work themselves out. Ms Thompson once said, 'No one will ever replace him, not for me, not for anyone who knew him, not for the entire world. It was an oddity, his dying at the same age as his mother and only two days beyond the date that she died on. It was as if she had reached out and pulled him on through.' She also quotes Elvis as often using Patton's line (out of the George C Scott movie) where he says, 'All glory is fleeting.' 'Elvis,' she said, 'knew that to be true.'

Indeed, his relationship with Linda, too, was fleeting and as it crumbled in the fall of 1976, he began seeing Ginger Alden. The tabloids, of course, sizzled in January 1977 when he gave her a $50,000 diamond ring.

Elvis had proposed to her, less than two months after they met, in the lounge of the bathroom at Graceland. Elvis literally got on his knees to ask Miss Alden to marry him and when she said yes, he pulled out a green velvet box with the 11.5 carat ring in it. Ginger remembered Elvis for his generosity and the fact that he was so easy to please. 'When he saw a lot of happiness in someone's face that was enough for him,' she observed.

Despite his detractors, from which he could escape, and his own pain, from which he could not, Elvis managed to wring

The Las Vegas Hilton was Elvis' home away from home for just over 30 weeks between January 1971 and December 1976. Over the years, Elvis' costumes became more and more ornate, until they began to resemble those of Elvis' piano-playing marquée mate in the photo *below*, taken in 1975. The photo *at right* was taken in 1972, during the filming of MGM's *Elvis on Tour*.

some measure of happiness from his relationship with Ginger Alden. Indeed, his role in that relationship paralleled the boyish impulsiveness of his early years with Priscilla. The night after they met he had taken her to see one of his planes at the Memphis Aero. After a short look inside, Elvis suggested they go for a ride. Ginger thought this was to be to Nashville, but several hours later she called her mother from Las Vegas.

Even bad or sensationalist news about Elvis Presley was profitable, however. The *National Enquirer* ran a story entitled 'Elvis' Bizarre Behavior and Secret Facelift' when it received word through the grapevine of the June 1975 surgery at Mid-South Hospital in Memphis. This issue went on to break all previous sales records for the magazine.

By 1976, however, the beginning of the end had come. Elvis had gained a great deal of weight and his physical appearance hardly fit his image. Colonel Parker became concerned about Elvis' actions on stage: he would forget lyrics and had to resort to using sheet music, he would ignore the audience and played instead to the band, shows were having to be cancelled and it was almost impossible to predict whether he would appear on stage or not. However, amid all the bad press, his records were selling in greater numbers than they had for several years.

In Great Britain, RCA Records had reissued 16 Elvis singles simultaneously. They included 'Return to Sender,' 'Jailhouse Rock,' 'It's Now or Never' and 'All Shook Up.' All 16 went on to the British charts immediately.

The last single to be released in Elvis' lifetime was 'Way Down.' It was a hit on the Easy Listening, Country and Popular charts and was followed by the album 'Moody Blue.' The RCA press release for this final album said:

'The album will initially be released as a limited edition, pressed on blue, translucent vinyl with a sticker calling attention to the fact that "Way Down" is contained in the album.

'RCA's blitz campaign on the single and album began in the trades and will continue there and in consumer publications through the months of June and July with special emphasis in cities Elvis will be visiting on tour and where the single is having the greatest market impact.

'Marketing aids will include two radio spots, one featuring "Moody Blue" and "Way Down" and the other featuring "Moody Blue" and Elvis' entire RCA catalog on which a special program will be running throughout the summer.

'A five-foot stand up display of Elvis will be the chief accessory among the merchandising items. Others will be a "Way Down" streamer, a "Moody Blue" poster featuring a blowup of the album cover, Elvis calendars and a die-cut display.

'Heavy advertising, window and in-store campaigns and other special localized promotions, are planned throughout the campaign.'

Even to the end, Elvis' talent never faded—but his reliance on it did. He began wearing increasingly flamboyant costumes emblazoned with rhinestones, studs and fringes. There were capes and huge matching belt buckles—all of which at times

These pages: **The power and intensity that the King brought to his concerts never diminished during nearly eight years on the road.**

added 35 to 40 pounds to his own weight. Some said he was beginning to look like Liberace.

In that final year Elvis kept up an incredibly gruelling concert schedule. Beginning on 12 February 1977, he played 50 cities before his final performance at the Market Square Arena in Indianapolis, Indiana on 26 June. It was the concluding performance of a 10 day stint of one night stands and it was, providentially, one of his best. The concert began with the usual 'Also Sprach Zarathustra' opening which segued into 'CC Rider.' After this Elvis teased with the crowd and slid into 'I Got a Woman.' During the one hour and 17 minute performance he gave his last audience 'Jailhouse Rock,' 'Teddy Bear,' 'Hound Dog,' 'I Can't Stop Loving You,' 'Bridge Over Troubled Water' and 'Hurt.' At least a dozen scarves were tossed to the adoring fans close to the stage. He then introduced each member of his backup band as well as his father, Ginger Alden, her mother and sister, his doctor, his three cousins, his sound engineers and his producer. He gave credit to everyone, and most of all, his audience, saying at the last that 'We couldn't have asked for a better audience and you have really made it worthwhile.' His final song was 'Can't Help Falling in Love' with which he unknowingly closed his tumultuous career.

The prescription drug noose which Elvis had drawn about his neck for many years finally drew taut on 16 August 1977, the day before he was to begin a 12-day sold-out concert tour. He had played racquet ball with friends until about 6:00 am, before retiring to the palatial bedroom at Graceland that he had been sharing with Ginger Alden. When they both awoke at around 9:00 am, little could Ginger realize that their ensuing pillow talk would be her last conversation with Elvis. Between 2:15 and 2:30 pm Alan Strada, one of his staff members, found Elvis sprawled face down and fully clothed on the floor of his bathroom. Strada summoned Elvis' road manager, Joe Esposito, and together they began applying mouth to mouth resuscitation and cardiac massage. Esposito called for a Fire Department ambulance and one was sent. The paramedics continued cardiac massage en route to Baptist Memorial Hospital. Dr George Nichopoulous met the ambulance at the hospital, and having noticed that Elvis' eyes were not yet dilated (indicating that he may still have been alive) he led a 40 minute effort to revive the fallen King. It was to no avail. At 4:00 pm Elvis Aron Presley was pronounced dead.

A group of six pathologists began an autopsy which was completed shortly before 8:00 pm. The body was then released to the funeral home. The medical examiner reported that 'There was severe cardiovascular disease present. He had a history of mild hypertension and some mild coronary artery disease. These two diseases may be responsible for cardiac arrhythmia, but the precise cause was not determined. Basically it was a natural death. The precise cause of death may never be discovered.'

The faithful began flocking to the gates of Graceland hoping to hear good news from within—hoping to hear that it was a mistake, an angry vicious rumor. But it was not to be. The King was dead. He died forever young and he will live in our hearts forever, but as darkness fell across the poplars lining Elvis Presley Boulevard on the evening of 16 August 1977, the King was gone.

In happier times: Backstage with his dad *(below)*, and filming his 1970 special *Elvis: That's the Way It Is (at right)*. Vernon Presley would outlive his famous son by nearly two years.

ELVIS
The King Remembered

On the day after Elvis died, the Memphis weather report called for a 60% chance of thunder showers with a high of near 90 degrees. It was to have been a typical hot August day in the South, but 17 August 1977 became far from typical. The headline in the *Memphis Press-Scimitar* stated that 'a lonely life had ended on Elvis Presley boulevard' and that Memphis would lead the world in mourning the monarch of rock and roll. The 'King' was dead, having lived just 42 years 7 months and 8 days.

When Elvis had been pronounced dead of a heart attack at 3:30 pm the previous day, many nurses and other attendants at Baptist Memorial hospital were overcome with grief. When his mother had died, 19 years and two days before, a sobbing Elvis had said before leaving the burial site 'Goodbye, darling, goodbye—I loved you so much.' Now the universal audience of mourners which gathered outside Graceland were in effect saying the same thing to him.

Elvis' health had deteriorated over the years, and he had been treated at Baptist Memorial Hospital from 28 January to 14 February 1975 for a chronic colon condition. Then on 1 April 1977 he was again admitted, this time with intestinal flu and gastroenteritis. Elvis had a history of giving gifts to hospital employees following stays at the facility. It was against hospital policy to allow such gifts and although the administration did not encourage it, Elvis was special. At one time he gave a nurse, Marian Cocke, a Pontiac Grand Prix because he 'knew how expensive it is to keep up a Cadillac.'

Immediately after Elvis' death was announced, telephone exchanges in Memphis were tied up continuously. A Western Union spokesman confirmed that at least 150 operators were put on duty spending all of their time on telegrams destined for Memphis. The Memphis paper had to add 50,000 extra copies to its normal circulation after callers flooded switchboards with requests. The main ingredient in most peoples' reactions to Elvis' sudden death was simple shock.

Below: The gates of Graceland. This 13.7 acre estate, located at 3764 Elvis Presley Boulevard (it used to be simply Highway 51 South) in Memphis, receives half a million visitors annually. The home on the estate, located a block from the gate, is constructed of tan Tennessee limestone and has 23 rooms. Elvis purchased it on 19 March 1957 from Mrs Ruth Moore, as a gift for his mother. He paid $102,500 for it then, but today it is worth (conservatively) a half million, although for its value as a continuing memorial to the King of Rock n' Roll, it is priceless! The bust *at right*, near the front doors of the Graceland mansion, is not an exact likeness of Elvis, but is more an impression of his spirit.

Everyone wanted to know more details, as they recalled all the good that the King of Rock and Roll had done—not only for the city of Memphis, but for the world in general.

Priscilla's father expressed his great shock by recalling that the last time he had seen Elvis was at a family Christmas party where Elvis had seemed jovial and happy. 'I had no idea that something like this would be happening so soon,' he said. Doctor George Nichopoulous, Elvis' private physician, had thought of asking Elvis to cancel his upcoming tour, but had decided against it because he felt that Elvis would have gone ahead anyway. Charley Rich, a long time friend, remembered the first time he had met Elvis—at the fairgrounds where Elvis had rented the entire place out and was taking poor kids on all the rides. Jerry Lee Lewis, Elvis' old colleague from his Sun Records days two decades earlier, expressed his own sadness at Elvis' death by saying, 'Elvis was one of the best friends that I had. I was shocked at his death. I cried because we lost the "King" of rock and roll. I believe the whole world will be shocked. We lost one of the greatest entertainers of all.'

At six minutes past noon on 17 August 1977, Elvis came home to Graceland for the last time—past throngs of mourners who waited for this last homecoming. 'Elvis is really dead. Why did he have to leave us?' someone asked. Others observed that they had come too late. Many mourners hoped that Graceland would be kept as a memorial to Elvis and resolved that if money were needed, people all over the world would help. Some outside the gates even passed out free coffee to other mourners, saying that it was all they could do for Elvis now. Another mourner commented, 'The vibes are too heavy, he's still alive somehow.'

People gathered at Graceland because it was the only way for common people to pay their respects. Many mourners kept saying that someone would come out and tell them that it was all a big mistake and that Elvis was not really dead, but that news never came.

Air National Guardsmen, police and firemen had to man the gates of Graceland mansion to control the thousands of weeping fans gathered to mourn Elvis' death. The gates were opened at 3:00 pm on the 17th to allow fans to view the body in the foyer of his home.

Elvis lay in state in Graceland inside a 900 pound copper lined coffin—wearing a white suit, a light blue shirt and a white tie. Tributes poured in from around the world. Frank Sinatra said, 'We lost a good friend,' Pat Boone commented, 'There's no way to measure the impact he made on society or the void that he leaves.' President Jimmy Carter issued a statement saying that Elvis' death 'deprives our country of a part of itself.' The President observed that Elvis' music and personality had 'permanently changed the face of American popular culture.' Flags were lowered to half staff throughout Mississippi and Tennessee as well as many other locations. A private funeral service was conducted in the Graceland music room for Elvis. Priscilla was present, as well as his father Vernon and daughter Lisa Marie. George Hamilton and Ann-Margret were also there as, of course, was Colonel Parker.

A number of spirituals were sung, including 'My Heavenly Father Watches Over Me,' 'Known Only to Him,' 'How Great Thou Art,' 'His Hand in Mine' and 'Sweet, Sweet Spirit.'

Graceland was scheduled to be closed at 5:00 pm but because of the surging crowds, family members allowed the gate to remain open until 6:30. When the time arrived, the hopes of many vanished as a solid wall of policemen closed the gates against the last-minute surge. An officer with a bull horn asked the crowd to disperse but his request was met with chants of 'No, No, No' and 'One more hour.' Deputy police chief John Molnar said an estimated 100,000 persons visited Graceland during that day to pay their respects. He said as many as 20,000 were in the area at one time.

Between 150 and 200 people had been given medical care by late afternoon. Most were women who had fainted from the heat and the press of the straining multitude while others had collapsed from exhaustion. Police observers noted that even though the crowds had been somewhat rowdy outside the gates, once they were admitted inside they were calm, quiet and somber. One girl expressed the feelings of many when she said 'I don't want this to be the last time in my mind, him lying there. I'd rather remember him standing up there glorious, but I have to see him. I won't believe it until I do.' The room where Elvis lay in state was heavily guarded and mourners were ushered out almost as soon as they had entered. Many were crying when they entered and most wept openly when they came out.

Elvis' funeral services were held Thursday afternoon in the music room at Graceland with the Reverend CW Bradley of the Wood Dale Church of Christ giving the funeral sermon. Following are excerpts from his address:

'Words do not take away from a man's life, and words do not add to a man's life in the sight of God. Though I will make several personal observations regarding Elvis, and from them seek to encourage us, it is not my purpose to try to eulogize him. This is being done by thousands throughout the world.

'We are here to honor the memory of a man loved by millions. Elvis can serve as an inspiring example of the great potential of one human being who has strong desire and unfailing determination. From total obscurity Elvis rose to world fame. His name is a household word in every nook and corner of this Earth. Though idolized by millions and forced to be protected from the crowds, Elvis never lost his desire to stay in close touch with humanity.

'In a society that has talked so much about the generation gap, the closeness of Elvis and his father and his constant dependence upon Vernon's counsel was heartwarming to observe. Elvis never forgot his family. In a thousand ways he showed his great love for them.

'In a world where so many pressures are brought upon us to lose our identity, to be lost in the masses, Elvis dared to be different...Elvis was different and no one else can ever be exactly like him. Wherever and whenever his voice was heard, everybody knew that was Elvis Presley.

'But Elvis was a frail human being. And he would be the first to admit his weaknesses. Perhaps because of his rapid rise to fame and fortune he was thrown into temptations that some never experience. Elvis would not want anyone to think that he had no flaws or faults. But now that he's gone, I find it more helpful to remember his good qualities.

'We are here to offer comfort and encouragement to Elvis' family. There is much encouragement in all the beautiful flowers sent by loving hands and hearts from around the world. There is much encouragement in the presence of so many who have crowded into our city in addition to those here. And also from knowing that literally millions throughout

At right: Gravesites of the Presley family. An estimated 100,000 mourning fans visited Graceland on the day of Elvis' funeral.

the Earth have their hearts turned in this direction at this hour. There is also much encouragement from the beautiful music. But the Greatest comfort and strength come from knowing there is a God in Heaven who looks down upon us with love and compassion and who says, "I will never leave you or forsake you."

'May these moments of quiet and thoughtful meditation and reflection on Elvis' life serve to help us also reflect upon our own lives and to re-examine our own lives. And may these moments help us to reset our compasses. All of us sometimes get going in the wrong direction.'

The white Cadillac hearse that took Elvis' body down Elvis Presley Boulevard to the cemetery was followed by 17 white Cadillac limousines. Over 100 vans were needed to transport literally tons of flowers to his final resting place. The day after his interment over 50,000 fans visited the cemetery and, at the Presley family's wish, each was asked to take a single flower in remembrance of Elvis. His pallbearers were Jerry Schilling, Joe Esposito, George Klein, LaMar Fike, Billy Smith, Charlie Hodge, Doctor Nichopoulous and Gene Smith. The funeral procession which pulled out of Graceland and headed down Elvis Presley Boulevard toward the cemetery was composed of 49 white Cadillacs, and was flanked by motorcycle police on the sides and helicopters overhead. The sheer persistence of the loyal mourners moved Police Director E Winslow Chapman to comment 'There's nothing like an Elvis fan.' Even though a few arrests were made, the crowds were fairly orderly considering their size.

While thousands thronged Memphis on the day of Elvis' funeral, a crowd of about 500 gathered quietly at his Tupelo, Mississippi birthplace for a short tribute. A local minister eulogized him by saying 'We thank God for the life of Elvis Presley, for letting him come our way, even in Tupelo on his journey in life and throughout the world.' The mayor of Tupelo declared Thursday an official day of mourning and that Elvis' birthday, 8 January, would be officially celebrated thereafter as Elvis Presley Day.

The flower shops in Memphis were swamped with so much business, they had to call in vacation help to fill orders which poured in from around the world. Fans sent orders ranging from one rose in a bud vase to elaborate designs costing over $500. To their credit, area florists coordinated the flowers in an orderly and attractive manner to give the funeral an appearance of dignity rather than a circus type atmosphere. One Ohio couple had been sending a $25 arrangement to be placed on Elvis' mother's grave once a month since her death in 1958, and when Elvis died they ordered the same for him. Even with an armada of vans to transfer the enormous field of flowers from Graceland to the Cemetery, it still took the florists and their helpers over five hours to complete the job. Floral arrangements came from such notable recording stars as Glen Campbell, the Carpenters, Elton John and Donna Fargo. Tennessee Governor Blanton also sent an arrangement. So did the Memphis Police Association and virtually every fan club from across the United States and Canada.

Memphis florists had flowers shipped in from California and Michigan to meet the staggering demand. The majority of requests were for red, yellow and pink roses. Also included were baskets, wreaths and vase arrangements. After the funeral more than 20 professional florists volunteered to strip the 3116 floral arrangements that were spread on the mausoleum lawn. The florists would have given each fan a single flower at the request of the Presley family, but the first

These pages: The biggest hit-maker in pop history. This long corridor wall in the Graceland mansion is full of Elvis' many, many platinum and gold records. Do you remember 'Heartbreak Hotel,' 'Mystery Train,' 'Hound Dog' and 'Love Me Tender?' How about such later hits as 'In the Ghetto' or 'If I Can Dream?' He had 38 Top Ten hits between 1955 and 1980—five more than the Beatles, who were themselves inspired by him.

93

fans who had arrived wanted more. They left with bouquets of orange and purple bird-of-paradise, chrysanthemums, carnations, roses and ferns—so that by mid day following the funeral only pieces of ribbon and styrofoam remained. The Professional Florists Association of Memphis even set up a 'flower policy' for handling future floral tributes to Elvis on his birthdays and other special occasions. Every limousine in Memphis was booked, and over 100 appeared at the funeral.

Over 50,000 visitors passed through the gates—most took home a souvenir of some kind. Traffic was bumper to bumper from a half a mile north of the cemetery gates south to Graceland, a distance of over three miles. One mourner said, 'People say he's just rock and roll but he did it all. He was a part of you, like a member of your own family. I've cried as much for him as for any family member.' Another commented, 'Why couldn't it have been me instead or anyone in this crowd? Why him?' Still another said, 'It was like somebody had cut out a piece of my heart.'

A plaque commemorating Elvis' achievements in karate was placed inside Elvis' crypt. It said: 'Tiger, Master Of The Art, presented to Elvis Presley, 8th Degree Black Belt.' (Actually Elvis had achieved the 9th Degree during the last year of his life.) There were reports that three women had 'offered their bodies' as inducements to enter the cemetery during the funeral, and that one out-of-town newsman had offered a cemetery employee $500 for a picture of the casket being taken into the crypt, but for the most part things could not have gone better, under the circumstances.

Many fans not only wanted flowers but also pictures of the Graceland mansion, but the gates were closed to visitors shortly after the funeral. Many would have been sent away disappointed were it not for Vester Presley, Elvis' uncle who was in charge of security at Graceland. He collected fans' cameras, took them inside the gates, took a picture of the mansion with each one, and then returned them to their owners. The Elvis magic was a family affair to the very end.

Wilbert McGhee, 66, was the cemetery worker who prepared Elvis' crypt. McGhee reflected: 'With him such a young man and me so old, it seemed funny that I opened a crypt for him.' He could remember a number of times when Elvis came riding up to his mother's grave on a motorcycle, usually with a pretty girl. 'He always smiled and waved. He seemed like he had a smile for everyone.'

Elvis Presley officially became history at exactly 4:30 pm on Thursday the 18th, when he was entombed in a grey marble crypt that was nine feet long by 27 inches high at Forest Hills Cemetery in midtown. His seamless copper coffin blanketed with rosebuds was wheeled into the crypt room of Corridor Z and lifted into place. His father, Vernon, wearing a black pin striped suit, stood for a moment with his hand on his son's coffin, and had to be supported by friends as he turned away.

Shortly after the entombment, the mausoleum was cleared and five workers entered the room with a wheelbarrow full of sand, a five gallon bucket of water, cement and a box of tools. They sealed the crypt first with a double slab of concrete, and then with marble. Security arrangements around the mausoleum at Forest Hills began to break down almost immediately, and soon thereafter Elvis' body was removed to Graceland where the meditation garden became his final resting place.

A few days after the funeral, Elvis' father, Vernon, searched for words to thank the world for its concern.

These pages: Part of the fabulous collection of Presley memorabilia at Graceland. Much of this having been the personal effects of the King himself, Elvis fans come here year round to muse over the mementos of a legendary life.

95

'It lightened my grief somewhat as I watched the tributes to my son that were shown from people throughout the world. But as everyone must know, I would rather have my son Elvis.

'I am very sorry that all of the people who came to Memphis were not able to view the body, but there was not enough time,' he said. 'I was afraid that it would become more dangerous as the night wore on for safety of the thousands of people that had come to Memphis to pay their tributes. I would like to express my sincere and deepest sympathy to the families of the girls in the very unfortunate and regrettable thing that happened at the gate. We want the families to understand.' (Two women had died after being hit by an automobile while standing in a no traffic area.)

'The funeral arrangements were all handled beautifully. I would like to thank the Shelby County Sheriff's Department, the Memphis Police Department and other officers for the way they handled all of the traffic problems.'

For hundreds of journalists from all over the world who covered the funeral, Presley said: 'You were most gracious. It is hard for me to put into words my thought at this time. But I do want you to know my feelings.

'I would like to take this opportunity to thank each member of the press, including the newspapers, radio, television and magazines, for their consideration to our family and friends during our sorrow after the death of my son, Elvis.

'Elvis did have a will and the attorneys will handle it next week. Elvis called me up to his suite at Graceland one night several months ago and asked me if I would have a will made up for him. We discussed it. Then I talked to the attorneys. It was drawn up. He approved it and it was signed and witnessed by three people and notarized.'

Elvis' final words to his father had been the on the previous Monday evening, less than 24 hours before his death. Vernon had told Elvis, 'I think I'll just go with you on this tour,' (meaning the upcoming series of one night stands to open in Portland, Maine that Wednesday night) and Elvis replied, 'Fine. The more the merrier.'

Because Elvis' death was so sudden, the tributes which poured in from around the world were more spontaneous in nature than the usual fare of funeral eulogizing. The Memphis Development Foundation issued a statement saying that it would introduce an Elvis Presley Memorial Fund to build a memorial to the entertainer. They noted that 'The city of Memphis is indebted to Elvis Presley. He gave much more than his talent to us. He gave us a legend, a dream, a success story that millions cling to. We owe him something. For this reason, the foundation would be honored to initiate and administer a memorial fund.'

Elvis Presley was a cop at heart. A former sheriff of Memphis recalled, 'He was just like a kid about law enforcement. He'd appreciate anything you could do for him in that line. He always wanted blue lights on his cars. In Las Vegas you could have some of the biggest personalities in the United States where Elvis could talk to them and you'd find him over in the corner talking to policemen.' Elvis had told the sheriff several times that if there was ever anything that law enforcement needed that he could do, he was always available. Elvis qualified to be a special deputy and had the authority to go armed and did so on many occasions. Elvis had great respect for his special deputy commission and never abused it.

At left: Fans pay their respects at Elvis' gravesite. Though possibly the most well-flowered grave in the US, the flowers keep coming.

Governer Edmund G 'Jerry' Brown, Jr of California issued a statement saying that Elvis had 'changed the face of American music. He had a significant impact on the culture and consciousness of America.' The governor also added, 'I spent a lot of time at the Heartbreak Hotel, and I used to have a pair of blue suede shoes.'

Elvis' generosity was infectious. In Heanor, England, Britain's official Elvis Presley fan club made plans to raise 500 pounds ($875) to buy a guide dog for the blind in memory of the star who made hound dogs famous. Elvis would certainly have approved of the idea.

Hotel and motel rooms in Memphis were booked solid through the funeral period, and Delta airlines added two extra flights from Atlanta to Memphis to help ease the demand. The Memphis Area Broadcasters Association issued a statement that all stations in that organization would devote 60 seconds of silence to Elvis' memory at 2:00 pm on the 18th.

The prestigious *Times of London* ran afoul of some readers when it commented on Elvis' death by dismissing him as an 'indifferent singer of mediocre songs and a totally uninteresting person.' Letters poured into the *Times* office demanding to know what other popular singers the newspaper considered to be superior to Presley, and wondering if the editors were simply unwilling to admit that any popular singers at all had any merit whatsoever. One irate fan wrote in: 'People did not buy Presley's records to annoy their parents—they bought them because they derived enormous pleasure from listing to his magnificent and unique artistic performances.' So it was with many who felt a great loss at his passing: somehow when Elvis died a part of their youth had died with him.

The delegates to the Tennessee Constitutional Convention unanimously adapted a resolution mourning Elvis' death, and praising him 'as an embassador of the highest quality from Tennessee to the world. Elvis Aron Presley will be remembered for the duration of the existence of the Earth for his benevolence, vitality, sensitivity and unique artistry.'

Tennessee Governor Blanton issued a statement praising Elvis as 'A great entertainer and great humanitarian who came from a sharecropper's son to be elevated by his own talent, his own ambitions, and his own generosity. His career was an American dream come true.' Mississippi Governor Finch declared a day of mourning for Elvis, and the state flag was ordered flown at half staff. In Tupelo, a special Elvis Presley Birthplace Memorial Trust was established by three local banks to finance a memorial to Presley in his boyhood home.

Joe Esposito, Elvis' road manager and friend for nearly 20 years, made a somewhat pointed observation in paying tribute to Elvis: 'All you read about Elvis is the bad things. I guess people like to read that kind of stuff but I don't know why. I hope everybody in the world that wrote anything bad about Elvis gets a good night's sleep.' He then suggested that one day all of Elvis' friends should put their experiences together and have writers assemble it into manuscript form and that would be the real story of Elvis Presley's life.

Sam Phillips of Sun Records recalled that even after Elvis left Sun for RCA Victor he still liked to come back to the Sun studios or to Phillips' house to sit and talk one on one. 'He'd come by to see me totally informally—on every occasion unannounced—and we'd go off together and sit and talk philosophy. Elvis called me in '68 from Vegas when he was preparing to make his long-awaited return to live appearances and he says, 'Mr. Phillips, I just got to have you come out. I'm scared to death. I got to have somebody I know, some friends in the audience.' Phillips thought that Elvis was truly frightened of being hurt.

Brian Wilson of the Beach Boys recalled how Elvis influenced that group and was a symbol for their generation. 'His music was the only thing exclusively ours. He wasn't my mom or dad's. His voice was a total miracle, a true miracle in the music business. It had an influence on the entire group.'

Cher commented, 'The first concert I ever attended was an Elvis Presley concert when I was 11 years old. Even at that age he made me realize the tremendous effect a performer could have on an audience.'

In Nashville, country music singer Hank Snow who helped arrange Elvis' first recording contract and counseled him in his early years said, 'I think if anybody deserved to be called a legend and a superstar it would be Elvis. He was very versatile; he covered the pop field, the middle of the road field, the blues field and, of course, earned the title King of Rock 'n Roll.' Even Tiny Tim, who was recording in Nashville at the time of Presley's death, issued a statement saying that 'Elvis leaves this generation without a singing star. It's very tragic.'

Elvis touched so many people from so many walks of life that it is not unreasonable to suppose that the best tributes to his life came from common fans. 'He was one of us; he wasn't no college kid.' 'It's something I can't explain, but I felt he was just an old country boy like the rest of us. There wasn't nothin' high fallutin' about him. When he sang it was like me and a friend singing. He might have had a lot of big stuff backing him up later on but when he sang it still came out country.' 'I'll tell you what I liked about him: Here was a guy from nowhere who came up and said, "Hey, I'm somebody." I like that. I feel like he came from the same roots that I came from. Us country boys always did stick together.'

Another fan said 'I love him and this is it. When this is over, (the funeral) there won't be no more. It's hard to believe. I seen him six times and I got tickets right now to see him in two weeks but that's out, now. But I'm not going to sell the tickets. I'll keep 'em as souvenirs. I got a lot of those. I got records, posters and a big oil painting on black velvet. Last night (Tuesday), me and two more Tupelo girls went to the house where he was born. We sat in the swing and I guess we were there three hours. I cried all night. Today (Wednesday), I had to come to Memphis. I can't really explain it. I probably won't get to see his body or anything. But at least I'll be here, you know? I'm from Tupelo and he's from Tupelo.'

'Me and a friend walked into a cigar store in Pittsburgh Tuesday night and heard the news on the radio. I'm an Elvis fan but my friend is even a bigger fan than me. I called the garage and asked them if I could take my week's vacation and they said yes and we drove all night, 800 miles, and we got in here this morning. Why did we come? Well, he's the king. He's the one and only. You don't see a king go out every day.'

'He meant a lot to me and I just couldn't pass this up. I think people loved him because he didn't change when he got to the top. He still helped little people out. I saw him 25 times. I saw him in Las Vegas, Dallas, Houston, Fort Worth and other places. He kissed me twice. I also got four of his scarves. I brought them along with me. I just graduated from school and I was going to move to Memphis in order to be able to follow him better. But now I won't come. I'll go back to Texas when all this is over. I feel sadder than I can say.'

'I wanted to come out and pay my respects because I enjoyed him and loved him like one of my sons. I saw him start out on the Ed Sullivan Show. I was in Akron, Ohio, then, and I

Tennessee's answer to King Tut's tomb. *Above:* The King of Rock n' Roll's multitudinous trophies in a stunning display at Graceland.

followed him ever since. I never was able to see him in person and that's why I came today. I thought I might finally get to see him. I feel like I lost a dear friend. I feel like Memphis has lost a friend and we will not have another one like him.'

When Elvis died the fans made an unprecedented run on his records in music stores across the nation. The Record Theatre in Buffalo, New York, which bills itself as the 'World's Largest Record Store' described the demand for Elvis records as 'unbelievable.' People were buying the complete catalogue of his records. His death made his recordings more popular—and many thought, more valuable. Stores scrambled to place orders with distributors for fresh albums, tapes and singles. One store reported selling over $700 worth of Presley albums within hours of the news of his death. On the day of Elvis' funeral, Colonel Parker asked Vernon to sign a contract that would extend his position as Elvis manager. The Colonel went to work immediately, keeping Elvis' name before the public with an 'ALWAYS ELVIS' campaign. After Elvis' death, RCA had to tie up every record pressing plant in the country to keep up with orders which amounted to over 200 million records in the first year. After that, RCA continued to release 'new Elvis albums,' and all went on the best seller lists.

He was six foot two inches with blue eyes and brown hair and a voracious appetite for hot dogs, blackeye peas and peanut butter and banana sandwiches. He was a lifelong fan of comic books with his favorites being Superman and Captain Marvel. In the early 60s, he helped raise over $100,000 in a benefit concert to raise funds for the USS Arizona Memorial commemorating the lives of those lost at Pearl Harbor in 1941. He never had a music or acting lesson in his life. He learned to play both the piano and the guitar totally by ear and for this became, in his era, the highest paid star in Hollywood. He used to call his mama 'Baby' and 'Darlin.' When he went into the US Army his serial number, 53310761, was memorized by millions of devoted female fans. He had 56 gold records, with total sales of 452,864,912 copies during his lifetime. 'Hound Dog' alone sold over seven million copies.

The only Grammy Elvis ever won was for his album 'How Great Thou Art' in 1967. However, he was the first artist in the history of the record business to top the three major charts: Pop, Rhythm and Blues and Country/Western. Elvis was no cruel and crass drug addict, but a Christian man who was a victim of his own love for his fans and their love for him.

One of the most tragic aspects of Elvis' death was that he was engaged to be married to Ginger Alden. 'It's like the whole world's at a standstill,' she said after the funeral. Elvis often took Miss Alden's family and sisters on tour with him and in the spring before he died, he took her to Hawaii for 10 days. Ironically it was at the Alden residence on Saturday night, 6 August 1977 that Elvis did his last singing. The singing was mostly religious hymns such as 'How Great Thou Art.' Elvis had planned to introduce Ginger on stage the Saturday night he was to have played Memphis during his upcoming tour. He told her to look 'real special.' The world was to officially be told that she was to become the next Mrs Elvis Presley. But that was never to be.

Elvis' will, probated before Judge Joseph Evans shortly after his death, made his father, Vernon, the executor of his vast fortune. Also present were Vernon's attorney, Beecher Smith II, his wife, Mrs Ann Dewey Smith, and Charlie Hodge—both of whom had also signed the will. Neither Priscilla, nor Ginger (who was the third of the three witnesses that signed the will when it was drawn up at Graceland on 3 March 1977), were named in the estate. Neither did Elvis name charitable organizations as beneficiaries. The instrument directed the elder Presley, then 62, to distribute the net income of the estate for the welfare of himself, Elvis' daughter Lisa Marie, and his grandmother, Mrs Minnie Mae Presley. According to the document, Vernon was to receive his son's personal property, including 'trophies and other items accumulated by me during my professional career.' He was also to have 'complete freedom and discretion as to disposal of any and all such property so long as he shall act in good faith and in the best interest of my estate.' The will also authorized Vernon to see to the health, education and welfare of 'such other relatives of mine living at the time of my death who in the absolute discretion of Vernon Presley are in need of emergency assistance.' Upon the deaths of either Vernon or Minnie Mae all remaining assets of the trust would go to Lisa Marie when she reached age 25. Included in the estate were five parcels of real estate in Shelby County (including Graceland) appraised in 1977 at more that $500,000. The will also stipulated that all royalties from the sale of Elvis' recordings and films were to be considered income for the trust. In granting Vernon Presley absolute control over the estate the will said: 'Any decision of the trustee as to whether or not distribution shall be made and also to the amount of such distribution shall be final and conclusive and not subject to question by any legatee or beneficiary hereunder.' That meant that Presley's father was allowed to hold or sell any real estate or other property, and permitted the use of any property such as houses or cars by any beneficiary without liability to himself. Interestingly, the

Above: Lisa Marie Presley and a friend at a gallery opening in 1987. A coincidence: Priscilla Presley is Jenna Wade on *Dallas* (*below,* with Steve Kanaly); Elvis was Jess Wade in *Charro*. *Opposite:* Priscilla's hairstyle—now its natural color—has changed since Elvis.

will under a 'spendthrift provision,' also says, 'any bequests contained herein for any female shall be for her sole and separate use free from the debts, contracts and controls of any husband she may ever have.'

Vernon Presley died on 26 June 1979 and left the bulk of his own estate to his girlfriend, Sandy Miller. Minnie Mae Presley died a year later in 1980, thus leaving Lisa Marie the sole surviving heir to the Presley fortune, which she will inherit in 1993 when she turns 25. By some estimations the Graceland estate alone is now worth $500 million. This, when combined with profits from the re-release of his albums on compact disc, could mean that Lisa Marie might inherit an estate worth over a *billion dollars*—even as situated on the Interstate that is today still a *very long way* from the east side of Tupelo, Mississippi, a town and a lifestyle that Lisa Marie will never know or understand.

Priscilla, still Lisa Marie's legal guardian, relocated to Los Angeles, and after signing with the William Morris Agency, became a national spokeswoman for Wella-Balsam hair products. Television commercials soon made Priscilla one of the most visible faces in America. During the late 1970s and early 1980s, she began serious acting studies with respected drama coach Milton Katselas, with whom she still studies. In addition to her pursuit of an acting career, she diversified and went into business with her personal dress designer, Olivia. The partners called their venture Bis and Beau, and for four years catered their exclusive designs to several stars including Barbra Streisand, Cher, Natalie Wood and Julie Christie. Priscilla sold her interest in the enterprise to Olivia.

Priscilla's dramatic film debut was in *Love is Forever* and her television debut came as co-host of ABC TV's *Those Amazing Animals* in 1979. In November of 1984 she returned

to Memphis to tape *Showtime's Tour of Graceland* which was broadcast in January of 1985. She holds a brown belt in Karate, which she finds the perfect exercise for keeping her body in tone. *Elvis and Me*, Priscilla's autobiography, was published by GP Putnam's in September 1985. The mass market paperback, issued a year later by Berkley Books, immediately went to the number one slot on the New York Times Best Seller list. The book was also made into an ABC-TV mini-series broadcast in February 1988. Priscilla is today most often seen in the role of Jenna Wade on the CBS TV series *Dallas*, a production of Lorimar Telepictures. She currently lives in Los Angeles with her fiance Marco Garibaldi and their son Navarone Anthony.

Lisa Marie Presley, who turned 21 in February 1989, was at one time portrayed by the press as having joined a cult. In 1988, meanwhile, she had announced her intention to marry her boyfriend, Kevin Dorian Jeffcoat, 22, and to name their first son after her famous father. The Graceland mansion, at 3764 Elvis Presley Boulevard in Memphis, is currently held in a trust fund as a part of the estate for Lisa Marie.

An average of 500,000 visitors per year come to Graceland to pay their respects to Elvis. In 1987 alone, the 10th anniversary of his death, over 608,000 fans from around the world made the pilgrimage to Graceland. It is conservatively estimated that this tourist business alone infuses over four million dollars a year into the Memphis economy. Elvis, even in death, still draws staggering crowds. How many *living* entertainers today can boast of performing for audiences of over half a million fans annually?

While her wedding dress stands on display at Graceland alongside headless mannequins wearing her late husband's most well-known stage clothes, Priscilla *(facing page)* has moved on to a new life. *Above:* Elvis' favorite guitars add to the clothing display, for the edification of the fans *(below)* who tour Graceland daily.

4E 77
ELVIS ARON PRESLEY

Elvis Presley was born in Tupelo, Mississippi on January 8, 1935, the son of Vernon and Gladys Presley. He moved to Memphis in 1948. Soon after signing a contract with Sun Records in 1954 he achieved tremendous popularity. His musical and acting career in records, movies, television, and concerts made him one of the most successful and outstanding entertainers in the world. He died on August 16, 1977 and is buried here at his Memphis home, Graceland.

These pages: A new generation comes to Graceland's wall. Born just two weeks before Elvis died, this young lady will come of age in a world forever changed by him.

By the time she accompanied her parents on their pilgrimage to Graceland, she had learned to know his music, and to acknowledge that there was only one King of Rock n' Roll.

It was Elvis' combination of black rhythm and blues and white country that became the rock n' roll that he pioneered. Both his music and his personality were unclassifiable. Elvis saw himself as an entertainer and not as anyone's vehicle for social change.

He was above the 'isms' of his day and in comparison to what came after him he remained, to the end, a 'clean cut kid— a nice young man.' People who become bigger-than-life usually have bigger-than-life trials and problems, but Elvis somehow managed to remain astonishingly clean and tame all his life. In an age of hard porn he was only suggestive. In an age of bloody violence he remained romantic and reverent. He was never vulgar or debasing. He believed in and acted the part of the authority figure. When the doctors told him that the drugs would not hurt him, he believed them because he had always been taught to believe those who were 'above him.' His detractors have portrayed his life as that of an emotional nomad living in a purposeless squalor, but he never pretended to be anything or anyone that he wasn't. He was Elvis.

He rode the edge of the wave of life, and ultimately found out where the limits really are. Within the confines of his spacious boredom he many times bumped his head on the ceiling and asked: Why can't I go any higher? Ultimately, he was released into that freedom.

His Southern upbringing provided his furthermost boundaries from the outset. The limits are somehow built into that milieu. When a country boy succeeds, most often he will eventually come to the point where he finds he cannot leap beyond that success. Perhaps for Elvis even religion became an object with which to nail down all the eventualities. If it became impossible for him to hold onto God, at least he could flit in and out of His shadow. It seemed as though his life was geared to show anyone who doubted it that he could make it— and more importantly make it all alone. Perhaps all of the hindrances should never have been taken so seriously after all.

The projections of his shimmering personality were fiery indeed, and most everyone always knew that he was hopelessly complete—almost another breed of human being. For such, *every* night is a Saturday night and *every* day is a Sunday.

Gratefully, the world, after Elvis, would never be the same.

Elvis ended one of his final concerts with the words: 'I hope I haven't bored you.'

No, Elvis, you didn't.

Index

A

Adams, Gerald Drayson: 53
Adams, Julie: 53
Albertson, Jack: 53
Alden, Ginger: 82, 84, 86, 99
Anders, Mary: 53
Aloha From Hawaii: 76, *76*
Andrew, Edward: 62
Andress, Ursula: 43
Ann-Margret: *35*, 46, *49*, 68, 90
Atlantic Records: 16
Ansara, Michael: 53

B

Balin, Ina: 60
Bad Nauheim, West Germany: 30
Austin, Pam: 46
Baptist Memorial Hospital: 70, 80, 88
The Beatles: 72
Beaulieu, Captain Paul: 30, 32, 66, 90
Beaulieu Presley, Priscilla: 30, 32, 37, 38, 66, 68, *68*, 70, *70*, 76, 79, 80, 84, 90, 99, 100, *100*, 103
Bergman, Alan and Marilyn: 60
Berlinger, Warren: 55
Betz, Carl: 55
Billboard: 14
Bixby, Bill: 55, 60
Blackman, Joan: 4
Blake, Bill: 14
Blanton, Tennessee Governor: 92, 97
Blue Hawaii: 4, *37*, 38, *41*, 55
Boone, Pat: 90
Bradley, Reverend CW: 90
Bronson, Charles: 41
Brown, California Governor Edmund G Jr: 97
Burton, Earl: 53

C

Callahan, Mushy: 41
Campbell, Glen: 92
Cardenas, Elsa: 43
Carpenter, Karen and Richard: 92
Carradine, John: 62
Carter, US President James Earl: 90
Cash, Johnny: 14, *14*
Change of Habit: 62
Chapman, E Winslow: 92
Charro: 60, *62*
Cher: 98, 100
Christie, Audrey: 55
Christie, Julie: 100
Clambake: 55, 66
Cocke, Marian: 88
Columbia Records: 16
Corey, Wendell: 25
Craig, Yvonne: *43*, 46
Crown Electric Company: 12, 14

D

Dallas: 100, 103
Day, Annette: 55
del Rio, Dolores: 37
Dorsey Brothers: 18
Double Trouble: 55
Douglas, Donna: 53
Douglas, James: 34
Douglas, Kirk: 34
Dylan, Bob: 72

E

East Heights Assembly of God Church: 8
East Tupelo, Mississippi: 8
Easy Come, Easy Go: 55
Eden, Barbara: *35*, 37
Egan, Richard: 20
Eisley, Anthony: 55
Elvis and Me: 32, 103
Elvis on Tour: 76, *83*
Elvis Presley Birthplace Memorial Trust: 97
Elvis: That's the Way It Is: 86, *111*
Elvis: What Happened?: 80
Esposito, Joe: 86, 92, 97

F

Fabares, Shelley: 53, 55
Fargo, Donna: 92
Faulkner, Edward: 53
Ferra, Sandy: *See* Sandy Martindale
Fike, LaMar: 92

Fike, Lenore: 30
Finck, Mississippi Governor: 97
Flaming Star: 35, 37
Follow That Dream: 41
Fort Chaffee, AR: 28
Fort Dix, NJ: 32
Fort Hood, TX: 28
Frank Sinatra's Welcome Home Party for Elvis Presley: 34
Frankie and Johnny: 53
Frankfurt, West Germany: 28
French, Victor: 60
Friedburg, West Germany: 28
Fun in Acapulco: 43, 66

G

Garibaldi, Marco: 103
Garibaldi, Navarone Anthony: 103
GI Blues: 6, 34, 37
Girl Happy: 53
Girls! Girls! Girls!: 41, 66
Gleason, James: 25
Godfrey, Arthur: 14
Goodwin, Laurel: 41
Gordon, Gale: 60
Graceland: 32, 37, *65*, 68, 75, 80, 82, 86, *89*, 90, 92, *92*, 94, 97, 99, 103
Grand Ole Opry: 14

H

Hagen, Ross: 60
A Hard Day's Night: 53
Hamilton, George: 90
Harrington, Pat: 55

Harum Scarum: 53
Help!: 53
Hawkins, Jimmy: 55
Heanor, England: 97
Heston, Charlton: 34
Hodge, Charlie: 92, 99
Holden, Jennifer: *109*
Holland, Danny: *100*
Holloway, Sterling: 58
Horn Lake, MS: 68
Houston Astrodome: 76
Hutchins, Will: 55

I

Immaculate Conception High School: 66
It Happened at the World's Fair: 41, 43
Ivers, Robert: 34

J

Jaffe, Nicole, 62
Jailhouse Rock: 24–25, 25, 28, 53, 55, *109*
Jeffcoat, Kevin Dorian: 103
Jeffries, Fran: 53
John, Elton: 92
Johnson, Rafer: 38
Jones, Anissa: 62
Jones, Dean: 25
Jones, Carolyn: *31*
Jordanaires: 23, 43, 53

Jurado, Katie: 58

K

Kanaly, Steve: *100*
Kanter, Hal: 22
Karey, Michele: 58, *60*
Katselas, Milton: 100
Kellogg, Lynn: 60
Kid Galahad: 41, 53, 60
King Creole: 26, 28, *31*, 53
Kiss My Firm But Pliant Lips: 58
Kissin' Cousins: 43, *43*, 46, 68
Klein, George: 92
Kovack, Nancy: 53, *53*

L

Lancaster, Burt: 34
Lanchester, Elsa: 55
Lane, Jocelyn: 53
Lange, Hope: 38
Langdon, Sue Ane: 55
Lansbury, Angela: 4
Las Vegas, NV: 70, 76, 84, 98
Las Vegas Hilton: 80, *83*
Las Vegas International Hotel: 7576
Lawhan Grade School: 8
Lawrence, Anthony: 55
Leigh, Suzanne: 51
Lelley, Joseph J: 43

Young Elvis. *These pages, from left to right:* Rocking out in the 1950s; musing intently amid several depictions of himself; as Vince Everett, with Jennifer Holden as Sherry Wilson in *Jailhouse Rock*; returning from Army service in Germany, with Colonel Parker.

Lennon, John: 72
Lewis, Jerry Lee: 14, *14*, 90
Live A Little, Love A Little: 58
Lockwood, Gary: 38
Long, Huey 'Kingfish': 18
Los Angeles, CA: 16, 100
Louisiana Hayride: 14, 17
Lowes State Theater: 10
Love is Forever: 100
Love Me Tender: 20
Loving You: 22–23, 25

M

McBain, Diane: 55
McCartney, Paul: 72
McGhee, Wilbert: 94
McGuire AFB, NJ: 32
MacLaine, Shirley: 34
Madison Square Garden: 76, 80
Maier, Sigrid: 34
Market Square Arena: 86
Marshall, Dodie: 55
Martindale, Sandra: 6, *7*, *7*, 34, 55
Martindale, Wink: *7*, *7*, 14
Marx Metal Products: 10
Mason, Marilyn: 62
Matthau, Walter: *31*
Memphis, TN: 10, 12, 14, 18, 28, 32, 70, 80, 92, 97, 98, 103
Memphis Area Broadcasters Association: 97
Memphis Police Association: 92
Memphis Press Scimitar: 88
Memphis Recording Services: 12, 14
Metro Goldwyn Mayer (MGM): 43, 75
Meredith, Burgess: 55, 58
Merrill, Gary: 55
Meyerink, Victoria: 60

Mid-South Hospital: 84
Miller, Hal: *29*
Miller, Sandy: 100
Milton Berle Show: 18
Mississippi-Alabama Fair and Dairy Show: 8, 22
Mobley, Mary Ann: 53
Molnar, John: 90
Montenegro, Hugo: 60
Moore, Mary Tyler: 62
Moore, Ruth: 89
Moore, Scotty: 14
Morgan, Harry: *53*, 55
Mullaney, Jack: 53, 55

N

Nadel, Arthur: 55
Nashville, TN: 14, 16, 38, 84, 98
Neal, Bob: 14
Nelson, Gene: 53
New York, NY: 16, 18, 76, 80
New York Times: 18
Nichopoulous, Dr George: 86, 90, 92
Nixon, President Richard: 79, *79*
North, Sheree: 62
Novello, Jay: 53

O

OC Hume High School: 10, 12
Odets, Clifford: 38

P

Paget, Deborah: 20, 22
Palm Springs, CA: 68
Paradise, Hawaiian Style: 38, 51, 55
Paramount Pictures: 18, 22, 38, 41
Parker, Col Tom: 18, 22, 30, *66*, 75–76, 80, 84, 90, 99, *109*
Pepper, Cynthia: 43, *46*
Perkins, Carl: 14, *14*, 16
Perkins, Millie: 38, *38*
Peters, Jon: 80
Phillips, Dewey: 14
Phillips, Sam: 14, 9798
Porter, Don: 58
Portland, ME: 97
Presley, Davada 'Dee': 37, 66
Presley, Gladys Love: 8, *10*, 12, 28
Presley, Jesse Garon: 89
Presley, Lisa Marie: 70, *70*, 79–80, 90, 99–100, *100*, 103
Presley, Minnie Mae: 30, 99–100
Presley, Vernon Elvis: 8, 10, *10*, 12, 30, 66, 86, *86*, 94, 97, 99–100
Price, Vincent: 62
Priest, Pat: 55
Professional Florists Association of Memphis: 94
Prowse, Juliet: 34

R

Rafferty, Chips: 55
RCA Victor: 14, 16, 18, 32, 84, 97
The Reno Brothers: *See Love Me Tender*
Rey, Alejandro: 43

Rich, Charley: 90
Robbins, Harold: 26
The Rolling Stones: 72
Roman, Yvonne: 55
Ronan, Leticia: 34
Rossington, Norman: 55
Roustabout: 53

S

Sahara Tahoe Hotel: 76
Sargent, Brooke: 58
Schallert, William: 60
Scott, Lizabeth: *23*, 25
Sgt Pepper's Lonely Hearts Club Band: 55
Shegata, James: 55
Showtime's Tour of Graceland: 103
Sidney, George: 46
Sinatra, Frank: 68, 75, 90
Sinatra, Nancy: 32, *32*, 58, 60
Smith, Ann Dewey: 99
Smith, Billy: 92
Smith, Gene: 92
Snow, Hank: 98
Speedway: 58, 60
Spinout: 55, 66
Springsteen, Bruce: 72
Stage Show: 18
Stanwyck, Barbara: 53
A Star is Born: 62, 80
Stay Away, Joe: 55
Stevens, Stella: 41
A Stone for Danny Fisher: 26
Strada, Alan: 86
Strauss, Robert: 55
Streisand, Barbra: 62, 80, 100
Sturges, Solomon: 60
Sullivan, Ed: 18

Sun Record Company: 12, 14, 16, 97

T

Talent Scouts: 14
Taurog, Norman: 38, 41
Tennessee Constitutional Convention: 97
Thompson, Linda: 80, 82
Those Amazing Animals: 100
Tickle Me: 53
Tiny Tim: 98
Times of London: 97
Tiu, Vicky: *41*, 43
Toast of the Town: 18
The Trouble with Girls: 60
Tupelo, MS: 910, 22, 92, 97, 98, 100
Tupelo Hardware Store: 10
Tyler, Judy: 2526, *28*

U

US Army: 26, 28, 30, 32, 99
USS *Arizona* Memorial: 99

V

Vallee, Rudy: 58
Van Paten, Joyce: 62
Viva Las Vegas: 46, *49*, 55, 68, *73*, 111

W

Walley, Deborah: 55
Wallis, Hal: 18, 20, 22, 34, 38, 41
Walters, Nancy: 4
Ward, Skip: 55
Weiss, Allan: 55
Weld, Tuesday: 38, *38*
WELO radio: 8
Werle, Barbara: 60
West, Red: 30, 80
West, Sonny: 80
WHBQ radio: 14
Whitman, Slim: 14
Wiere Brothers: 55
Wild in the Country: 38, 53
William Morris Agency: 100
Williams, Bill: 53
Williams, Hank: 14
Williams, John: 55
Wilson, Brian: 98
Wolfe, Lonnie: *29, 30*
Wood Dale Church of Christ: 90
Wood, Natalie: 100

XYZ

Yarnall, Celeste: 58
Zenoff, David: 68

These pages, left to right: Elvis lays a bet in *Viva Las Vegas*; relaxing after a performance in the early 1970s; in production on MGM's *Elvis: That's the Way It Is*; and Elvis 'live on stage' in the 1970s.

'He was a precious gift from God.'
—*the opening line of the inscription on his gravestone.*

Custer State Park's
Tatanka

Outdoor fun in 1998

Inside ...

Safety 3
Camping 4
Campsite Reservations 5
Park Volunteers 5
Bison 6
Park Wildlife 7
Special Events 8
Buffalo Roundup 9
Park History 10
Nature Programs 11
Park Trails 12-13
Scenic Drives 14
Lakes & Streams 15
Park Resources 16
Getting Around 17
Concessions 18
Resorts 19-22
Black Hills Playhouse 23
Park Map . . . . .Back Cover

Tatanka is published by the S.D. Game, Fish and Parks Dept. Division of Custer State Park

Tatanka is the Lakota word for bison or buffalo.

WILLIAM J. JANKLOW
Governor of South Dakota

JOHN COOPER
Game, Fish & Parks Secretary

ROLLIE NOEM
Custer State Park Director

SCOTT CARBONNEAU
Tatanka Editor

Volume 19, 1998

Game, Fish & Parks printed 200,000 copies of this publication at a cost of 10 cents each.

Welcome!

Welcome to South Dakota's Custer State Park! We're glad you are here and hope your visit is both pleasant and relaxing.

One of your first stops in the park should be our historic Peter Norbeck Visitor Center. This unique log and rock structure was built by the Civilian Conservation Corps and is listed on the National Register of Historic Places. The building also houses a host of interpretive displays that explain the area's diverse resources and geologic features.

If you're looking for a great place to stay, I hope you will visit one of the park's four resorts: the State Game Lodge, Sylvan Lake Lodge, Blue Bell Lodge and Legion Lake Resort. For more on these areas, turn to pages 19-22 of this publication.

The history buffs in your family will be sure to enjoy the Badger Hole, Gordon Stockade, Mount Coolidge Fire Tower and Black Hills Playhouse. All are located within the park's boundaries.

Other exciting attractions can be found in our neighboring communities. For additional information, please contact the following Chamber of Commerce offices:

Rollie Noem
Custer State Park Director

Custer Area, 800-992-9818; Hill City Area, 800-888-1798; Hot Springs Area, 800-325-6991; and Keystone Area Chamber of Commerce, at 800-843-1300.

We encourage you to experience all the Black Hills have to offer and hope to see you back soon!

Park Fees

ENTRANCE FEES
Annual Park Entrance License $20
Second Annual Park Entrance License $10
Transferable Park Entrance License $45
Temporary License (May 1 to Oct. 31) . . . .$3/person or $8/vehicle
Temporary License (Nov. 1 to April 30) . . . .$2/person or $5/vehicle
Motorcoach License . . . .$1/person per continuous visit

CAMPING FEES
Blue Bell, Sylvan Lake, Grace Coolidge, Legion Lake, Stockade Lake, Game Lodge and French Creek Horse campgrounds . . .$13 per camping unit
Center Lake Campground . . . .$10 per camping unit
French Creek Natural Area . . . .$2 per person/night
Game Lodge & Stockade group areas . . . .$2 per person/night

An entrance license is required of all park visitors. Only people traveling non-stop on U.S. Highway 16A and 87S are exempt from this requirement.

1998 Tatanka

Safety First!

We hope you enjoy your stay at Custer State Park. With any outdoor activities, however, there is a certain amount of risk involved. Please take a few minutes to read the following safety tips.

If an emergency should arise, please refer to the the appropriate emergency numbers listed on this page.

BISON - The park's biggest attraction is its herd of North American bison. But remember -- these animals are dangerous, so please give them plenty of space.

POISON IVY - Not everyone is allergic to poison ivy, but its reaction can be very uncomfortable. Learn to recognize this plant and wear long sleeves and pants when hiking in wooded areas or along streams.

TICKS - These tiny insects are found in thick vegetation. Ticks can spread Rocky Mountain spotted fever, Lyme disease and other illness. Care should be taken in removing ticks.

SNAKES - Custer State Park is home to the venomous prairie rattlesnake. The snake will strike if threatened, and treatment is required at the nearest medical facility.

WATER - Campers and hikers should NEVER drink water from lakes, streams or springs.

WEATHER - Thunderstorms are common in the Black Hills region. Lightning, hail, strong winds and heavy rains may be associated with these severe storms.

CLIMBING - Rock climbing should be done only under the supervision of trained instructors.

JUMPING - Visitors are not allowed to jump or dive from bridges, rocks or cliffs into any of the park's lakes, ponds or streams.

Bison can be dangerous and unpredictable ... please give them space

Important numbers!

We want your stay at Custer State Park to be safe and enjoyable. Please keep these numbers in a convenient location. Pay telephones are located at all resorts, most campgrounds and the Peter Norbeck and Wildlife Station visitor centers.

EMERGENCY
Mount Coolidge Fire Tower . . . .(605) 255-4567.

MEDICAL SERVICES
Rapid City Regional Hospital . . . .(605) 341-1000
Rapid City Regional Hospital Emergency Room . . . .(605) 341-8222
Custer Community Hospital . . . .(605) 673-2229
Custer Clinic . . . .(605) 673-4150
Urgent Care Clinic (Custer) . . . .(605) 673-3417
Poison Control Center 1-800-952-0123

LAW ENFORCEMENT
South Dakota Highway Patrol . . . .(605) 394-2286
Custer County Sheriff . . . .(605) 673-4467

OTHER
Campground Reservations 1-800-710-2267
Park Headquarters . . . .(605) 255-4515
Weather Information . . . .(605) 341-7531
Peter Norbeck Visitor Center . . . .(605) 255-4464
Wildlife Station Visitor Center . . . .(605) 255-4054
State Parks Web Page . . . . .www.state.sd.us/sdparks/

1998 Tatanka

Camping!

There's something for everyone at Custer State Park's seven designated campgrounds. Whether you're looking for a modern campground with a nearby resort or a campground with hiking trail access, we have a site to suit your needs.

Campsites

Each campsite at Custer State Park has a gravel or paved camping pad, a fire grate and picnic table. **Electric hookups are not available.**

Firewood may be purchased at most of Custer State Park's resort areas or convenience stores.

The park's modern campgrounds have flush toilets, while Center Lake's semi-modern campground has vault toilets. All areas have warm showers.

Evening programs are presented nightly at campground amphitheaters between Memorial Day and Labor Day. Program listings and other important information may be found on each of the campground bulletin boards.

About 200 campsites throughout the park may be reserved beginning Jan. 2 for the entire season, while other sites are available on a first-come basis. To reserve a campsite, call the central reservation center at 1-800-710-CAMP (2267).

Campgrounds with first-come sites include Stockade Lake South, Grace Coolidge and Center Lake. Campers who wish to stay on one of these first-come sites, should simply select a site that appears unoccupied or is not posted with a valid and current camping permit.

Camping fees are collected daily and are based on the number of camping units in your party. A camping unit is a powered vehicle, motorhome, camping bus, pull-type camper, tent or any other device designed for sleeping.

Minor children may camp on the same site as their parents, in a tent, without paying the daily camping fee.

In some areas throughout the park, a maximum of two camping units may occupy one site, but each unit will be charged a camping fee.

Enjoy your stay at one of Custer's seven campgrounds

Primitive Campsites

For a more rugged experience, two primitive campgrounds are found in the French Creek Natural Area. Hikers using this area for overnight stays must camp in the designated sites and bring their own water. Fires are allowed only in grates.

Self-registration fee stations are located on each end of the natural area. The fee is $2 per person, per night. More on this area is available at the Peter Norbeck Visitor Center, (605) 255-4464.

Group Camping

Custer State Park has two group campgrounds: one near Stockade Lake and the other adjacent to the Game Lodge Campground.

The Game Lodge Group area features showers, flush toilets, picnic tables, water, and fire grates on site. It is located near the Game Lodge Resort and the Peter Norbeck Visitor Center. Fishing, swimming, hiking, and Park Naturalist programs are all located within 1/4 mile of the campground.

The Stockade Lake Group camp is located on the shores of Stockade Lake. The area features vault toilets, fire grates, picnic tables and water on site. Showers and flush toilets are available within walking distance at the Stockade Lake South campground. Evening programs are presented nightly on the other side of the lake, in the Stockade North campground.

Reservations are required and can be made by contacting the Custer State Park Office at (605) 255-4515.

Horse Camps

The French Creek Horse Camp is designed specifically for campers with horses and reservations are required. It is located near Blue Bell Lodge and Resort, on CSP Road 4.

New in 1998 is a comfort station with flush toilets and showers! Limited corral space is also available at the camp. Horses are not allowed to graze and riders must bring their own feed. Beginning in 1999, all hay brought into the park must be certified weed free.

1998 Tatanka

Reserving Campsites

By dialing 1-800-710-2267, campers may reserve campsites throughout most campgrounds in the park.

Reserved campsites at Custer State Park are available between Memorial Day and October 10. Reservations are accepted for the entire camping season beginning January 2, or as few as two days before you arrive.

There is no reservation fee for South Dakota residents, but all non-residents are required to pay a non-refundable $5 processing fee.

To reserve a site, simply call 1-800-710-2267. The reservation center is open from 7 a.m. to 7 p.m. daily between Memorial Day and Labor Day. From Jan. 2 to May 24 and from Sept. 8 to Oct. 10, the reservation center is open from 7 a.m. to 5 p.m.

Camping fees for the entire stay must be paid when the reservation is made. Campers may pay by credit card, money order, gift certificate or personal check. All checks must be received within five days of making a reservation.

Checks may be sent to:
**State Park Reservations
523 E. Capitol Ave.
Pierre, SD 57501-3182**

A $10 cancellation fee or one night's camping fee (whichever is less) will be charged if you cancel any part of your reservation. All other camping fees will be refunded.

Reserved campsites are available in the following campgrounds by calling the toll-free reservation center at: 1-800-710-CAMP:

- ✓ Blue Bell
- ✓ Game Lodge
- ✓ Legion Lake
- ✓ Stockade Lake (north unit)
- ✓ Sylvan Lake
- ✓ French Creek Horse Camp

Camping Facilities

CAMPGROUNDS	Number of Sites	Fee / Night / Unit	Reservable Sites
Blue Bell Campground	35	$13	32
Center Lake Campground (2)	71	$10	0
Game Lodge Campground	57	$13	54
Grace Coolidge Campground (2)	26	$13	0
Legion Lake Campground	25	$13	22
Stockade Lake Campground (2)	68	$13	38
Sylvan Lake Campground	39	$13	36
SPECIALIZED CAMPING AREAS			
French Creek Natural Area		$2/person	0
Game Lodge Group Area**		$2/person	all
Horse Camp	31	$13	26
Stockade Group Area**		$2/person	all

- Within the campground
- ✓ Available within one mile

*Reservations available by calling 1-800-710-CAMP (2267)
** Reservations required

NOTE: After the comfort stations are closed for the season, a basic fee of $6 per night, per unit is charged.

Volunteers!

Campers interested in donating their time and energy will find Custer State Park an ideal place to spend either part or all of their summer months.

Volunteers can assist with staffing needs at the visitor centers, perform general park maintenance or act as campground hosts. Whether the task is small or large, each volunteer plays a very important role in Custer State Park and the many services it provides.

In return, volunteers receive a campsite with complete hookups. Anyone interested in volunteering should pick up a volunteer application at the Peter Norbeck Visitor Center.

Applications are also available by contacting:

**Custer State Park Volunteer Program
HC 83, Box 70
Custer, SD 57730-9705
(605) 255-4515**

Donations

Donations are always welcome at Custer State Park and may allocated to your favorite program. All donations are tax-deductible and should be made out to either Custer State Park or the S.D. Parks and Wildlife Foundation. Please rember to earmark your donation for resource management, visitor services or maintenance.

The Parks and Wildlife Foundation is located at: 523 E. Capitol Ave., Pierre, SD, 57501-3182, and may be reached by calling (605) 773-3387. Electronic mail inquiries may also be sent to the foundation at: susane@gfp.state.sd.us

Volunteers are important

The Bison!

Tatanka is the Lakota word for buffalo!

"Tatanka"

The sound of this Lakota word conjures images of a great vision, painting a picture of a time when this mighty beast ruled the Great Plains.

Hollywood movies, folklore and our own ideas create a personal vision of the tatanka or bison. The vision becomes real at Custer State Park, thanks to the foresight of early conservationists.

The North American bison was saved from near extinction during the early 20th century. The last bison in the Custer area was killed in 1884. In 1914, more than 30 bison from the Scotty Philip herd near Fort Pierre, South Dakota, were introduced to the Custer Game Preserve.

Those first bison were purchased by Philip from the Pete Dupree estate. Dupree captured several animals in the Grand River's last bison hunt in 1881.

Custer State Park's herd now totals 1,400. Between 400 to 500 calves are born each spring. These animals weigh about 65 pounds at birth and are reddish brown. Shortly after birth, the cow and calf return to the herd where the young play together and develop motor and social skills.

From July to September, older bulls rejoin the main herd and breeding season begins. This is an active time as bulls rival each other for breeding rights. Battles are furious and roars echo across the park's open grassland. <u>Watching the herd during rutting and calving seasons should only be done from the safety of your vehicle.</u>

Following the rutting season, adult males leave the herd and wander the park alone or in small bachelor groups.

When snow blankets the ground, bison use their short, flat noses as snowplows to expose the nutritious grasses below.

The tatanka vision is available to anyone visiting Custer State Park. To experience that vision first hand, drive along the Wildlife Loop Road and take the time to watch these majestic animals in their natural habitat.

After this experience, you will truly see a tatanka vision. May it never fade from your memory and may this vision always instill the value of wild things and the need to preserve them in natural settings such as Custer State Park.

Note: Bison are dangerous. Please view them from a safe distance!

Please don't feed us!

Feeding any of the park's wildlife is strictly prohibited!

In fact, feeding any wild animal can be dangerous to both yourself and the animal you are feeding.

Here are a few reasons to keep your food to yourself:

✓ Human foods, which are generally high in sodium and fat, pose great risk to wild animals. Species like prairie dogs derive all of their moisture from plants. When they eat human foods, their entire digestive system is altered.

✓ When animals are fed by humans, they may lose their fear of people. In turn, the animal may attack, bite or kick park visitors.

✓ Animals accustomed to begging and receiving food from passing vehicles may lose their fear of highways. This creates a dangerous situation and increases the possibility of car accidents which can injure both park visitors and park wildlife.

✓ When wildlife become dependent on human foods, they lose their willingness, and sometimes their ability, to secure their own natural foods.

✓ In some cases, park officials must eliminate sick animals that have been fed by humans. This is especially true when the animals' digestive systems are blocked with the inappropriate things they have eaten.

Please do your part to spread the "do not feed the wildlife" message.

Wildlife!

Many mammals, birds, amphibians and reptiles make their home in Custer State Park. Included are the following:

ELK
Elk are shy and seldom seen during the daytime hours. In South Dakota, they are found only in the Black Hills region. Elk are grazers, like cattle, and browsers, like deer. Adult bulls grow and shed heavy, wide antlers each year.

WHITETAIL DEER
Whitetails live mainly in the brush lands. As its name implies, the whitetail deer has white hair on the underside of its tail. When the animal runs, the tail is flipped up and looks like a waving flag.

MULE DEER
These deer are aptly named for their large ears. Their black-tipped tails, which are short and narrow, are carried down when the deer runs. Mule deer bound with a stiff-legged gait as if bouncing up and down on powerful springs.

PRONGHORN
Pronghorns live mainly on the open grasslands. The name "pronghorn" comes from the bucks' large prong-like horns. The female's horns are unpronged. These animals possess remarkable endurance and can run 40 miles per hour for great distances.

MOUNTAIN GOAT
The Rocky Mountain goat was not found in South Dakota until 1924, when it was introduced to the Black Hills region. Today, they are found in the Harney Peak, Needles and Mount Rushmore areas. The mountain goat is actually a mountain antelope and not a true goat. The all-white animal grows a dense wool undercoat and a long outer coat of hair. Both sexes have sharp, slender black horns.

Custer State Park is home to many creatures

BIGHORN SHEEP
South Dakota's original wild sheep was the Audubon bighorn. When it became extinct in 1920, a herd of Rocky Mountain bighorn sheep was introduced to Custer State Park. Bighorns have a sturdy, but graceful build. Their coat consists of short hair, not wool. Both rams and ewes have horns; the males' are thick and curled.

COYOTE
The coyote hunts on open prairies and fields. Its food consists mainly of small mammals, but it also eats insects, fruits and berries. The coyote is gray and has a drooping, bushy tail and a pointed nose. The wily coyote is also South Dakota's state animal.

PRAIRIE DOG
The black-tailed prairie dog is found on the dry, upland prairie. It is a rodent that lives in large social groups called towns. The round mound of dirt that surrounds the prairie dog hole keeps rain water from running into the burrow and serves as an observation post to watch for danger. Prairie dogs get their name from their bark-like call.

BIRDS
The park's diverse habitat makes it an exciting bird-watching area, where visitors can find the red crossbill, mountain bluebird, golden eagle, prairie falcon and western tanager. A free bird checklist is available at the park's visitor centers.

BIG CATS
Chiefly nocturnal and reclusive toward humans, mountain lions and bobcats are found within the Black Hills. Both prey upon other species, including rabbits, wild turkeys, deer and young elk. While they do not control the other species' populations, these big cats do contribute to South Dakota's wealth of wildlife.

Remember:

Please do not feed any of the wild animals found within Custer State Park. And be sure to keep your distance, as these are **WILD** animals!

Special Events

Come Join The Fun!

Spring Open House Weekend
May 16 & 17

Beginning 8 a.m. Saturday and ending 8 p.m. Sunday, park entrance fees will not be charged at any South Dakota state park or recreation area.

Free Fishing Weekend
May 16 & 17

Fishing licenses are not required in South Dakota throughout the weekend.

Buffalo Wallow Golf Tourney
May 16

You can't rollerskate in a buffalo herd, so how about a round of golf? This team/foursome best ball competition is held on a primitive course mapped out along the park's foot hills and rolling prairie. Entries are limited to the first 25 foursomes. Entry fees include tickets to an awards cook-out following the tournament. Contact the Game Lodge at (605) 255-4541 for more information.

Volksmarches

Volksmarches are non-competitive walks along pre-marked routes. Each of the events listed below are seasonal volkssporting events.

Peter Norbeck Visitor Center
May 16 to October 31

Wildlife Station Visitor Center
June 1 to September 28

Volksmarching is a great way to explore Custer State Park

National Trails Day
June 6

A 5K walk and race begins near the historic Gordon Stockade. Family hikes, nature walks and other trail events are planned at the park.

Buffalo Roundup Arts Festival
October 3-5

Be sure to join the many festivities associated with Custer State Park's annual Buffalo Roundup. This year's celebration includes an arts festival with exhibit booths, entertainment and chili cook-off.

The arts festival features artisans and craftsmen from around the region. Anyone interested in exhibiting their arts and crafts should contact the State Game Lodge at (605) 255-4541.

Buffalo Roundup
October 5

Join in the action as park staff, cowboys and cowgirls saddle up to move the park's 1,400 bison to the buffalo corrals. The roundup is held near the park's buffalo corrals, located in the sourthern part of the park, along the Wildlife Loop Road.

Buffalo Auction
November 21

The annual Buffalo Auction serves a vital role in controlling Custer State Park's bison herd. Surplus bison and burros are sold each year at the park's live auction beginning at 10 a.m. on the third Saturday in November. For more information contact the park office.

Recycle It!

Recycling is something many of you are familiar with, and it is very easy to do. It is frightening to think that last year Americans threw away more than 1 million tons of aluminum and 11 million tons of glass. All of this could have been recycled instead of taking up limited landfill space. Recycling would also drastically reduce the amount of raw materials and energy needed to produce new products.

Custer State Park has already started a program to help you recycle aluminum. The park provides containers to collect aluminum cans for recycling. Recycling bins for other materials are located in neighboring communities including Custer, Hermosa and Rapid City. If you have any questions regarding directions to the nearest bin, ask a state park employee.

Annual Buffalo Roundup

It's a crisp October morning and the songbirds are chirping. Dew glistens on the amber grasses, as a low rumble grows louder and louder. Suddenly, hundreds of bison stampede over a hilltop.

Each fall the wild west returns to Custer State Park during the annual Buffalo Roundup.

Park staff, cowboys and cowgirls saddle up to move the park's 1,400 bison to the buffalo corrals.

The 1998 roundup is October 5-8. The event is open to the public and is free of charge.

Custer State Park's buffalo roundup serves several purposes. The first is to move the entire herd into a system of corrals along the Wildlife Loop Road.

Once in the corrals, the animals are sorted by the park's resource personnel. Most of the bison are released back into the park, while others remain in the corrals until an auction that is held during the third weekend in November. The auction helps control the bison herd's numbers and provides a valuable source of income for South Dakota's Custer State Park.

Animals to be sold at the auction are tested for tuberculosis and brucellosis. All calves are branded and the female calves are vaccinated for brucellosis.

Revenue received from the annual buffalo auction remains in the park and comprises a portion of the park's annual operating budget.

For more information on the buffalo roundup or auction, please contact the park office at:

Custer State Park
HC 83, Box 70
Custer, SD 57730
(605) 255-4515

The buffalo roundup is an annual event!

Join The Crowd!

Join the crowd this fall at Custer State Park's 5th Annual Buffalo Roundup Arts Festival!

This three-day event will be held Oct. 3-5 in conjunction with the park's annual buffalo roundup. All activities take place near the Peter Norbeck Visitor Center and State Game Lodge, off U.S. 16A.

The arts festival features artisans and craftsmen from around the region. Start the morning off with a pancake and sausage breakfast and then browse through the many exhibit booths.

Entertainment is scheduled throughout the day and features local talent including: cloggers, square dancers, American Indian hoop dancers, jugglers and cowboy poets.

If you're looking for something really exciting, be sure to watch modern day gun slingers compete in a fast draw competition or witness the re-enactment of the hanging of Fly Speck Billy!

The arts festival is also the site of the annual Custer County Chamber of Commerce Chili Cook-off. Chili chefs keep all of their ingredients a secret, but each batch of chili must use buffalo meat!

Chefs from around the area brew up their favorite recipe and spectators are invited to sample as many entries as their mouths can handle. Most chefs charge only 10 cents per sample.

If the thought of mouth-burning chili turns your stomach, then be sure try a world-famous buffalo burger or sample something else hot off our grills!

Several special events are scheduled throughout the day, so be sure to join the crowd, relax and enjoy the beautiful fall scenery and activities at the Buffalo Roundup Arts Festival.

A day at the Arts Festival!

1998 Tatanka

Park History!

The Gordon Stockade

In the summer of 1874, an expedition led by Lt. Colonel George A. Custer discovered gold in the Black Hills. Under the Treaty of Fort Laramie, however, this region belonged to the Plains Indians and white settlement was not allowed.

Word of the discovery spread quickly and a group of gold seekers from Sioux City, Iowa, moved into the Black Hills that following winter. Upon their arrival, the Gordon Party built a log fortress on the banks of the French Creek to protect themselves from possible Lakota attack.

The Gordon Party's stay was short, not very profitable and within five months they were removed from the hills by the U.S. Cavalry.

Following their eviction, a flow of fortune seekers came to these newly-discovered mountains of gold. It was more than the army could control and within two years, nearly 10,000 white people inhabited the Black Hills.

Today's Gordon Stockade is a replica on the original site. A sign near the gate tells the history and significance of the site.

Each summer, a living history program is held near the Stockade. This program shows the daily life of settlers in the 1870s.

Demonstrations include gold panning, roasting and grinding coffee beans, woodworking and cooking over an open fire.

The living history program is offered from 10 a.m. to 4 p.m. Mondays, Thursdays and Saturdays from mid-June through mid-August.

Guided tours are offered daily at Badger Clark's home

The Badger Hole

There's a cabin in Custer State Park affectionately known as the Badger Hole. This cabin was home to one of the park's most colorful characters.

Charles "Badger" Clark was South Dakota's first and only poet laureate. He lived in the park for the last 30 years of his life. The stories of Badger Clark, his life and poetry are stories of a man living an independent life.

Clark built his home, the Badger Hole, near Legion Lake. From within this cabin, he wrote poetry, read from his extensive library and wrote letters to his many fans. He lived there until his death in 1957, at the age of 74.

His life was fulfilling, as he enjoyed people and people enjoyed him. He gave lectures, told stories and recited his poetry at many social gatherings.

His distinctive dress -- riding breeches and boots, military blouse, flowing tie, officer-type jacket and broad-brimmed hat -- illustrated the independence and mystery of this bigger-than-life man.

Today, the Badger Hole remains much as it was when Badger lived there. As you walk through the doors of the Badger Hole, or wander along the Badger Clark Historic Trail, you walk back into a place and a time of a man who lived and shared a simple life.

A second cabin, adjacent to the Badger Hole, is open to the public. This cabin was Badger's home while he built the Badger Hole.

Each of the cabins are open daily to the public for tours from Memorial Day to Labor Day. The hours are:

10 a.m. to 5 p.m.

Staffing and upkeep of the Badger Hole is accomplished with the dedicated assistance of the non-profit Badger Clark Memorial Society.

Note: For more information on Badger Clark and his works, please stop at the Peter Norbeck Visitor Center.

Nature Activities!

The Jr. Naturalist Program is designed especially for kids!

Family Activities

Custer State Park's interpretive program has an assortment of activities that allow visitors the opportunity to explore, discover, learn and experience the beauty of South Dakota's Black Hills. These programs are conducted between Memorial Day and Labor Day, and focus specifically on the region's natural and cultural history.

EVENING PROGRAMS

Every evening, programs are presented in four of the park's campgrounds: Blue Bell, Center Lake, Game Lodge and Stockade Lake. These programs range from outdoor cooking demonstrations, where you'll have the chance to try some tasty recipes, to educational slide presentations with environmental themes.

INTERPRETIVE NATURE WALKS

Naturalists guide visitors through open grasslands, dense forests and towering granite spires, exposing them to the natural world around us. These walks provide an excellent opportunity to learn more about the park's birds, wildflowers, wildlife, geology and history. Participants are encouraged to wear sturdy footwear and dress appropriately.

PATIO ACTIVITIES

Imagine playing a habitat game with your children or studying the unique traits of mammals while making plaster casts of their tracks. These activities, along with others, are held throughout the summer on the front patio of the visitor centers.

HOOK-EM & COOK-EM

Grab your fishing equipment and enjoy the summer sun while testing your luck in one of the park's lakes or streams. Park naturalists reveal the secrets of fishing in the Black Hills and the natural history of the region's aquatic life. A valid South Dakota fishing license is required.

The Peter Norbeck Visitor Center is open 8 a.m. to 8 p.m. daily between Memorial Day and Labor Day; and from 9 a.m. to 5 p.m. between May 1 and Memorial Day; and between Labor Day and Oct. 31.

The Wildlife Station Visitor Center is open 10 a.m. to 7 p.m. between June 1 and Labor Day; and 10 a.m. to 5 p.m. from Labor Day to Sept. 30.

Learning made fun!

A variety of programs are designed especially for the park's younger visitors. Each will provide greater insight into the world around them.

JR. NATURALIST PROGRAM

South Dakota's Junior Naturalist Program is a vacation highlight for many who visit Custer State Park. The program teaches children 7-12 about the natural world surrounding them and provides them with hands-on environmental education.

Participants may request a Junior Naturalist participation card at any of the entrance stations or visitor centers. They must then attend three park activities, one of which must be a Junior Naturalist Hour. At the end of each activity, the child must have a park naturalist sign their card.

Once the card is completed, the new Junior Naturalists are awarded a certificate and colorful patch. They are then encouraged to share their new knowledge with other children.

Each Junior Naturalist Hour is limited to 15 participants. The program is open to all children and parents are asked to attend the awards ceremony.

ECHOES PROGRAM

Everyone Chooses How Our Earth Survives (ECHOES) is a free environmental education program for children 13-15 or those who have completed the Jr. Naturalist Program.

The goal of ECHOES is to teach children how to care for the Earth's natural and cultural resources.

To complete the ECHOES program, children must complete four special activities. Upon completion, participants will receive an ECHOES certificate and embroidered patch. An ECHOES brochure is available at either of the park's visitor centers.

1998 Tatanka

Happy Trails...

Custer State Park offers a variety of different hiking experiences. By parking their car and hitting the trails, visitors will discover this scenic area from a new perspective.

The park's trails vary in length and difficulty. Bicycles are allowed on most park trails. A general bicycle and hiking trail brochure is available at visitor centers and entrance stations.

A Historic Trail

A stroll down memory lane may be just the ticket for a lazy summer day. This trail highlights historical features found in the area.

✓ Badger Clark Historic Trail is a one-mile tribute to South Dakota's first poet-laureate. The trail wanders behind Clark's historic cabin, the Badger Hole, and follows rocky hillsides, scenic vistas and pine forests. This was Clark's favorite area and inspired many of his poems. A brochure featuring his poetry is available at the Badger Hole and visitor centers.

Interpretive Trails

These trails offer insight to the natural world around us. Interpretive brochures or signs convey points of interest along the trails. The free brochures are available at the park's visitor centers.

✓ Sylvan Lake Shore Trail is the easiest of Custer State Park's hiking trails. The 1-mile path makes a complete loop around Sylvan Lake. Gigantic granite boulders line portions of the lakeshore and make Sylvan the most picturesque lake in the Black Hills. Look for interpretive signs along the trail.

✓ Prairie Trail is a 3-mile path that crosses the open grasslands. This area is prime habitat for bison, pronghorn and coyote. The trailhead is adjacent to the Wildlife Loop Road, 4 miles south of the Wildlife Station Visitor Center, 12.5 miles from the State Game Lodge or 5.5 miles from the Blue Bell entrance station. Be sure to pick up a free copy of the trail brochure at the park's visitor centers.

✓ Sunday Gulch Trail offers an outstanding hike with diverse scenery. The 2.8-mile trek includes an awesome gulch that swallows the entire valley below. The path forks to the left just below the Sylvan Lake Dam and follows a babbling stream. In 1971, the loop was designated a National Recreation Trail. Interpretive brochures are available at the visitor centers.

Several scenic trails cross through Custer State Park

Pick up a trail guide today

Other Hiking Trails

These self-guided loops range from 1.5 to 3 miles long. Trailhead signs are located at the start of each trail. A hiking trail brochure is available at the park's visitor centers, entrance stations or park headquarters.

✓ Lover's Leap Trail is 3 miles long and begins behind the park's historic schoolhouse, just west of the State Game Lodge and Resort.

✓ Stockade Lake Trail starts one-third of a mile from U.S. Highway 16A on the Stockade Lake Drive. This 1.5-mile trail displays part of Custer State Park's extensive timber management program.

Natural Area Trails

Little development has taken place in the park's natural areas. The trails are worn paths that follow streams.

✓ French Creek Natural Area is a 12-mile path through one of the most scenic gorges in the Black Hills. The trail follows the meandering French Creek, past limestone cliffs, placid pools and a forest of pine and oak.

This is not a looped trail, and visitors will find trailheads on either end of the 12-mile stretch. The west entrance is 3.1 miles east of Blue Bell Campground on CSP 4. The east entrance is 3.8 miles south of the State Game Lodge on Wildlife Loop Road.

✓ Walk-In Fishing Area Trail features 3 miles of backwoods delight. This trail follows Grace Coolidge Creek and lies between the Center Lake Dam and the Grace Coolidge Campground. This is not a looped trail. The northern trailhead lies adjacent to the Center Lake shower house and the southern trailhead is across the road from Grace Coolidge Campground.

Specialized Trails

These trails offer scenic diversity and are marked with blazed numbers, blue or gray diamonds or brown fiberglass posts.

✓ Cathedral Spires Trail spans Custer State Park's mountainous country. Granite peaks and outcroppings are found around every turn. Camping is not allowed in this area, which features three trailheads: Sylvan Lake Day Use Area; Little Devil's Tower parking area (1 mile south of Sylvan Lake on the Needles Highway); and the Cathedral Spires parking area (3.5 miles south of Sylvan Lake on the Needles Highway).

✓ Harney Peak is the country's highest point east of the Rocky Mountains. It lies in the Black Elk Wilderness Area within the Black Hills National Forest. Several trailheads for the Harney Peak trail system are found within Custer State Park. A popular trailhead is near the Sylvan Lake Day Use area.

✓ The Centennial Trail stretches 111 miles from Bear Butte State Park to Wind Cave National Park. More than 20 miles of the trail passes through Custer State Park. Area trailheads include: Camp Remington/Needles Highway, Badger Hole and French Creek Horse Camp.

Camping areas within the park include Legion Lake, Horse Camp and West French Creek.

Information on this trail is found in the park's trail brochure, available at entrance stations and at visitor centers.

✓ The 110-mile George S. Mickelson Trail does not run through Custer State Park, but trailheads may be found within the city of Custer and at nearby Hill City.

The George S. Mickelson Trail is currently under construction. Trail users are asked to avoid using trail sections that are not completed and open to the public.

Sections of the trail that are open to the public include a 42-mile stretch between Pringle and Hill City; and an 20-mile segment between Deadwood and Dumont.

Completion of the entire 110-mile stretch is slated for October of 1998. Trail passes are available at self-registration stations along the path. **Pedestrians are not required to purchase a trail pass.**

Be sure to pack your canteen

Etiquette and Safety

Hiking is a lot of fun and a healthy outdoor activity. To ensure you have a safe and pleasant hike, please remember the following safety and etiquette tips:

* Water is not available along the trails. Always carry your own supply in a reusable container.

* Camping within Custer State Park is only allowed in designated campgrounds.

* Open fires in both Custer State Park and the Black Hills National Forest are allowed only in designated fire grates.

* Please pack out what you pack in. Collect litter along the trails and dispose it when you return to camp.

* Always be aware of weather conditions. Afternoon thunderstorms are common in the summer months.

* Be sure to leave a message with someone describing the trails you will be hiking, with an estimated time of your return.

* Trails are marked with blue diamonds and orange blazers. The Centennial Trail is marked with gray diamonds and brown fiberglass posts.

* Poison ivy is often found along trails, especially near streams.

* Custer State Park is home to one of the largest publicly-owned bison herds in the world. These are wild animals, so please keep your distance if you should encounter one along any of the park's hiking trails.

* Although they are uncommon in the Black Hills, rattlesnakes are sometimes seen in Custer State Park. Please be on the lookout.

1998 Tatanka

Scenic Drives!

A drive along the Peter Norbeck Scenic Byway

Mt. Coolidge Lookout

The Mount Coolidge Lookout and Fire Tower was built in 1940 by the Civilian Conservation Corps. It rests atop a 6,023-foot peak and is used for communications and spotting fires.

The turnoff is located on SD 87. A 1-mile gravel road leads visitors to the top of the mountain, but large motorhomes and vehicles should avoid making the trip, as the road is narrow and winding.

From the top, visitors can see as far away as the Badlands!

For a real adventure ...

There's nothing like a leisurely ride along Custer State Park's three scenic drives: the Needles Highway, Wildlife Loop Road and Iron Mountain Road.

These winding drives are enjoyed at a slower pace. Please allow ample time to travel at a safe speed -- generally 25 miles-per-hour or slower.

NEEDLES HIGHWAY

The Needles Highway is more than a 14-mile road -- it's a spectacular drive spanning pine and spruce forests, meadows surrounded by birch and aspen and rugged granite mountains.

The road is named for the Needles rock formations. These tall, pointed columns seem to reach for the sky and resemble sharp, granite needles.

The roadway was carefully planned by former South Dakota Governor Peter Norbeck, who marked the entire course on foot and by horseback.

Traveling down this road, visitors pass the picturesque waters of Sylvan Lake. A short distance from the lake is a unique rock formation. Wind, rain, freezing and thawing created the opening that gives this boulder its name -- the Needle's Eye.

WILDLIFE LOOP ROAD

The Wildlife Road takes visitors through the park's open grasslands and pine-speckled hills. The 18-mile drive passes through an area that is home to many of the park's wildlife.

Animals often seen along this drive include: pronghorn, bison, whitetail and mule deer, elk, coyote, burros, prairie dogs, eagles, hawks and a variety of other birds. The best times for viewing wildlife are in the morning and evening when most animals are active.

The Wildlife Station Visitor Center is located on the southeast part of this loop. Visitors will find shade, information, mounts and outdoor habitat exhibits.

IRON MOUNTAIN ROAD

This winding road runs between Mount Rushmore and the junction of U.S. 16A and S.D. 36. Although only a portion of this road lies within Custer State Park, it is a must-see route.

Along the highway are wildfire exhibits, pigtail bridges, pulloffs with magnificent Black Hills scenery and tunnels framing Mount Rushmore.

On the Custer State Park section is a small group of the park's burros.

PETER NORBECK SCENIC BYWAY

Complementing the park's three scenic drives is the Peter Norbeck Scenic Byway. This includes some of the most dramatic natural and historic features in the Black Hills.

Sites include the Needles, Mount Rushmore and a bird's eye view of the area's rocky peaks and forested hills of the Black Hills National Forest.

This designated scenic byway includes all or portions of two scenic drives within the park. The byway was named for former South Dakota Governor Peter Norbeck who planned and surveyed most of the roads located within the park.

14   1998 Tatanka

Lakes & Streams!

Custer State Park features four mountain lakes with resort facilities and countless mountain streams. These areas are a major hub of activity during the summer months, with such popular activities as fishing, boating and swimming.

Below is a run-down on these popular lake and stream activities:

Fishing

Fishing is allowed anywhere in Custer State Park, but a valid South Dakota fishing license is required.

Anglers will find rainbow, brown and brook trout in the park's waters. The daily limit for trout is five per day and 10 in your possession. Only one trout can exceed 14 inches, but there is no minimum size restriction.

It is legal to use artificial lures, flies, worms or other bait, and minnows can not be used except on Stockade Lake. A variety of sport and pan fish are found in Stockade Lake including bass, perch, crappie, trout and bullhead.

Licenses, bait and tackle are available at each of the four resort areas; license fees are at right. For daily limits and rules, please refer to the 1998 Fishing Handbook, available at the park office or visitor centers.

Try your luck on one of Custer State Park's lakes and streams

1998 Fishing License Fee Schedule

License	Resident	Non-Resident
One-Day	N/A	$9
5-day	N/A	$29
Annual	$9 (plus $5 basic license)	$49
Family	N/A	$59

Boating

Boating is permitted within Custer State Park, with the following restrictions:

Sylvan Lake - No motorized boats.
Legion Lake - No motorized boats.
Stockade Lake - All boats allowed.
Center Lake - Only small motors and slow, non-wake boating is allowed.

Non-motorized boats more than 12 feet and all motorized boats, regardless of length, are required to have a valid boat license from South Dakota or another state.

Swimming

Swimming is allowed at the park's four beaches: Center Lake, Legion Lake, Sylvan Lake and the Game Lodge Pond.

There are no lifeguards and jumping from cliffs and rocks into the water is strictly prohibited. Pets and glass containers are also prohibited from all zoned swimming beaches.

For your safety, be sure to wear a personal flotation device (life jacket) whenever you are in the water. Personal flotation devices are mandatory for all people riding in a boat on South Dakota waters.

Limits

The following fishing limits are in effect on all South Dakota waters:

Fish	Daily	Possession
Perch	25	50
Crappie	25	50
Trout	5	10
Bullhead	100	200
Walleye	4	8
Northern	6	12

The possession limit is the number of fish any licensed angler may possess at any given time.

1998 Tatanka

Park Resources!

A valuable asset

Custer State Park's most valuable asset is its natural resources. So it's no surprise a great deal of time and planning is spent each year to ensure those resources are productive and protected.

Staff members at Custer State Park recently completed a new resource management plan. The planning effort used a holistic style to include two levels of public involvement.

First, a focus group was established to review current issues, establish goals and assist park staff in reviewing proposals for the future of Custer State Park's resources.

Then, meetings were held across the state to gather public input. The plan encompasses the years 1995 - 2010 and utilizes GIS (geographic information systems) technology to generate computerized maps.

The new plan includes a revised resource program mission statement, in the form of a holistic three-part goal describing the quality of life, the expected production and the future landscape descriptions of the park's natural resources.

Landscapes are described in three ecological systems: mixed grasslands, forest lands and water ecosystems. Future management directions are also highlighted for resource management activities.

To review a copy of the Custer State Park Resource Management Plan for 1995-2010, please visit the Custer or Rapid City city libraries.

Our most valuable asset ... the land

Fees help support Custer State Park

Custer State Park is unique among state parks throughout the country for many reasons. The fact that it supports itself places it in a category all its own.

The park's day-to-day operations are entirely financed through funds generated by the park itself. Most of these funds come from the sale of entrance licenses, surplus timber and bison sales, camping receipts and resort franchise fees. Revenue generated from these sources funds routine maintenance, resource management, visitor programs and park administration. The park's philosophy is, "Those who use the park, its facilities and programs should help in its operation and upkeep."

In some instances, major projects including sewer and water systems, have received funding from the South Dakota Legislature. In addition, the park's four resorts have been improved with revenue bonds paid by concession franchise fees. Improvements made possible through this program include: new log cabins at Blue Bell Resort, an addition at Sylvan Lake Lodge, renovation to stores at Legion and Sylvan Lake Resorts, remodeling of motel and cabin units and employee housing.

In many respects, Custer State Park is operated like a business. Budgets are based on projected revenues. If these revenues fall short of projections, the budget is readjusted

Camping and entrance fees are very important

accordingly. When the park generates more assets than projected, those funds are saved for the future.

Park staff are dedicated to preserving and protecting the park's natural and cultural resources, as well as offering a quality experience. The goal is to accomplish these objectives without placing the burden on the state's taxpayers. The support of park visitors in this effort is very important and much appreciated.

Thank you for supporting Custer State Park!

Getting Around!

Traveling through Custer State Park is not as difficult as it may seem. By looking at the map on the back page, visitors can easily determine where they are and where they would like to be.

It is important, however, that visitors watch their odometer and not their watch. Winding roads make travel through Custer State Park much slower than in other areas of the state. Please plan all travels accordingly.

If you ever have questions regarding your location within Custer State Park, please feel free to stop any passing park employees or stop at the nearest visitor center or resort.

The visitor centers also have current South Dakota highway maps and maps of the outlying regions. The visitor centers are located near the State Game Lodge and along Wildlife Loop Road.

How Far Is It?

From the Peter Norbeck Visitor Center

Badger Hole (via US 16A)	.6 miles
Badlands National Park	88 miles
Black Hills Playhouse (via US 16A & SD 87N)	.9 miles
Blue Bell (via the Wildlife Loop Road)	20 miles
Center Lake (via US 16A & SD 87N)	10 miles
Custer (via US 16A)	15 miles
Gordon Stockade (via US 16A)	11 miles
Hermosa (via US 16A & SD 36)	14 miles
Jewel Cave National Monument (via US 16A & US 16)	28 miles
Legion Lake (via US 16A)	.6 miles
Mount Coolidge Fire Tower (via US 16A & SD 87S)	.9 miles
Mount Rushmore National Memorial (via US 16A N)	20 miles
Rapid City (via US 16A, SD 36 & SD 79)	28 miles
State Game Lodge	1/8 mile
Sylvan Lake (via the Needles highway - SD 87N)	19 miles
Wind Cave National Park	23 miles
Custer Battlefield National Historic Site, Montana	286 miles
Devil's Tower, Wyoming	140 miles
Glacier National Park, Montana	770 miles
Yellowstone National Park, Wyoming	441 miles

Tunnels are found on three highways in or near Custer State Park. Drivers of travel trailers, campers, recreational vehicles and buses should be aware of the tunnel sizes. The numbers correspond to the tunnels shown on the back map.

Tunnel Information

Iron Mountain Road—US 16A N
- ❶ 12'6" (3.8m) High   13'6" (4.1m) Wide   Has by-pass
- ❷ 12'6" (3.8m) High   13'6" (4.1m) Wide   Has by-pass
- ❸ 12'6" (3.8m) High   13'6" (4.1m) Wide   No by-pass

Sylvan Lake Road—SD 87/89, North of Sylvan Lake
- ❹ 10'8" (3.3m) High   10'0" (3.0m) Wide   No by-pass

Needles Highway—SD 87 N
- ❺ 11'5" (3.5m) High   8'7" (2.6m) Wide   No by-pass
- ❻ 12'0" (3.7m) High   9'0" (2.7m) Wide   No by-pass

Travel is slow ... plan your journeys accordingly

Custer State Park Airport
Elevation 3980 ft.
Unattended
No Fuel
Pay Telephone
Pilot Shelter

CUSTER STATE PARK RESORT COMPANY

Plan your trail ride by calling Blue Bell Resort today

There's lots to do at Custer State Park's four resort areas. The following are favorites among our many visitors.

Hayride/Chuck Wagon Cookout
Blue Bell Resort

This old fashioned hayride, on a vehicle-drawn wagon, takes you on a scenic ride along the park's back roads. The journey eventually takes you to a beautiful mountain meadow canyon for a Chuck Wagon feast.

Sing-alongs and country/folk music entertains throughout the evening. A true Western Adventure!

Reservations are required by 2 p.m. Late reservations and walk-ons will be accommodated on a "space available" basis until 5 p.m. Participants should arrive at Blue Bell Lodge by 5 p.m. for a 5:30 p.m. departure. The evening ends back at the lodge at approximately 8 p.m.

Menu choice of 8 oz. choice sirloin steak or 1/3 lb. hamburger entrée with all the fixin's including cowboy beans, cornbread and honey, potato salad, cole slaw, watermelon, cookies, chuck wagon coffee and lemonade. A souvenir cowboy hat and bandanna are afforded each paying guest. Infants 3 and younger are free, provided they sit on a parent's lap on the ride and eat from a parent's plate. Group rates for 10 or more people.

Trail Rides
Blue Bell Stables

Saddle-up and hit the trail for horseback adventure along the park's historic Indian trails. It's an exciting way to see some scenic areas. Rides include:
- One-Hour
- Two-Hour
- Half-Day (includes lunch).
- Full-Day (includes lunch).
- Overnight Pack Trip

During the overnight trips, riders relive the Old West with campfire meals and tent camping under the stars. Everything is provided, just bring a jacket, camera and imagination.

Note: Children must ride alone and meet minimum safety requirements. Please arrive 30 minutes before a scheduled ride to complete the required insurance-related paperwork.

Boat and Water Sport Rentals
Sylvan Lake & Legion Lake

Explore the solitude of a mountain lake or race your friends across the water in a paddleboat, rowboat, kayak or hydrobike.

All persons under 18 years must have an adult sign for the rental and have adult supervision while in the water. Life jackets are furnished and required.

Mountain Bike Rentals
Legion Lake

Two-wheel adventure for the whole family. The 111-mile Centennial Trail passes through the Legion Lake area!

Buffalo Safari Jeep Ride
State Game Lodge

Get set for adventure and have your camera ready with this 1 1/2 to 2-hour scenic tour of Custer State Park's back country. The driver/guides offer historical and educational information on the park and its wildlife as they take you on a ride of a lifetime. Departing 8a.m. to 6 p.m. daily. Reservations recommended. Group rates available for parties of 10 or more.

Dinner Theater Experience
Black Hills Playhouse

Make a dinner reservation at one of our beautiful resorts and receive Black Hills Playhouse ticket reservations with the same call. Simply call the lodge of your choice for reservations, and your tickets will be waiting when you arrive for dinner. Please make all reservations at least 48 hours in advance.

Custer State Park Resort Co.
HC 83, Box 74
Custer, SD 57730
(605) 255-4772
Reservations: 1-800-658-3530
www.custerresorts.com
email@custerresorts.com

Custer State Park Resort Company, a subsidiary of Wild Phil's, Inc., of Custer, SD, is an authorized concessionaire of South Dakota's Dept. of Game, Fish and Parks, serving the public in Custer State Park.

1998 Tatanka

STATE GAME LODGE
CUSTER STATE PARK

This gracious stone and wood lodge is set in a beautiful mountain valley, surrounded by a ponderosa pine forest. Grace Coolidge Creek winds through the valley and offers excellent trout fishing. Oak, birch and aspen trees line the babbling creek, providing a colorful year-round display.

The State Game Lodge and Resort served as the "Summer White House" for President Calvin Coolidge in 1927 and was visited by President Dwight D. Eisenhower for several days in 1953. It was built in 1920, and is now listed on the National Register of Historic Places.

ACCOMMODATIONS at the State Game Lodge include well-appointed motel units and pine-shaded cabins. Housekeeping cabins with kitchens or kitchenettes and sleeping cabins are also available.

Meeting and banquet rooms are available for family reunions and small business conferences. Please check with our staff at any of the Game Lodge facilities for assistance in planning your upcoming special events.

The Game Lodge was built in 1920

Pick up snacks at the Coolidge General Store

THE PHEASANT DINING ROOM offers a feast of native game, chef's specialties and many other fine entrees. This historic dining room is open from 7 a.m. to 9 p.m. daily during the summer months.

Enjoy your favorite cocktail, cappuccino, latte or espresso at our inviting lounge, just off the main lobby. Then, be sure to admire our historic photographs and ornate fireplace.

BUFFALO SAFARI JEEP RIDES provide a great adventure leading you from the State Game Lodge to the park's back country. Don't miss this exciting open air jeep ride in search of wildlife, with educational and historic commentary. Reservations are recommended for this 90-minute to two-hour adventure.

THE COOLIDGE GENERAL STORE and Gift Shop is located just beyond the chapel, one-quarter mile west of the Game Lodge. This unique store offers grocery and deli items, fishing licenses, gasoline, camping supplies and souvenirs. In 1927, shipbuilders from Minnesota built this complex to accommodate the entourage of staff, reporters and curious tourists that followed President Coolidge. The builders used their ingenuity to engineer a ceiling which resembles the hull of a ship turned upside down. The Coolidge General Store is a historic structure with a wide assortment of gifts and merchandise. The General Store and Gift Shop is open from 7 a.m. to 9 p.m. daily.

THE GAME LODGE CHAPEL is located adjacent to the Coolidge General Store and holds non-denominational Sunday services at 8:30 a.m. and 10:30 a.m., June through August. The Chapel is also available for weddings and other special events.

AN ARTIST IN-RESIDENCE will be working on new pieces throughout the summer in the the Game Lodge lobby. Some works of art will be available for sale.

For more information on the State Game Lodge call:
(605) 255-4541

Sylvan Lake Resort

Enjoy all the comforts of home at Sylvan Lake Resort

Rich in history and natural beauty, Sylvan Lake holds the designation of Custer State Park's "crown jewel." The lake was created in 1881, when Theodore Reder built a dam across Sunday Gulch. In 1921, this unique lake became a part of the newly-created Custer State Park.

In 1895, a Victorian-style hotel opened its doors on the shores of Sylvan Lake. The hotel was a popular site for many Black Hills vacationers until it burned to the ground in 1935.

The current hotel was opened in 1937, and the new wing was added in 1991. The hotel features cozy lodge rooms, a lobby, lounge and restaurant. Several rustic cabins in the area are nestled among the pine and spruce forest.

THE LAKOTA DINING ROOM is open from 7 a.m. to 9 p.m. daily during the summer months and features native game entrees and seafood specialties. Relax in the lounge adjacent to the dining room, lobby and veranda. Piano music is provided as evening entertainment.

SYLVAN LAKE GENERAL STORE is open from 7 a.m. to 9 p.m. daily during the summer months and offers fast food service, groceries and a large selection of gifts and souvenirs. Camping supplies, fishing licenses and bait are available for the outdoor adventurer.

A large patio overlooks the lake and is great for those afternoon snack breaks!

PADDLE BOATS, rowboats, hydro-bikes and kayaks can be rented for 30-minute, half-day and full-day excursions on beautiful Sylvan Lake. Life jackets are provided. Get your exercise while exploring a beautiful mountain lake!

THE SYLVAN LAKE AUDITORIUM, located adjacent to the Sylvan Lake General Store, is ideal for family reunions, receptions and other group functions.

THE VERANDA CHAPEL, located near Sylvan Lake, offers non-denominational services each Sunday, beginning at 9 a.m. between June and August.

AN ARTIST IN-RESIDENCE will be working on new pieces throughout the summer in the the Sylvan Lake Resort lobby. In addition to visiting with our guests, the artists will have some works of art available for sale.

OTHER ACTIVITIES including fishing, swimming, boating, hiking and rock climbing are available near the Sylvan Lake area. The Sunday Gulch, Sylvan Lake Shore and Harney Peak trails offer diverse opportunities for exploring the area. The Sunday Gulch Trail was designated a National Recreation Trail in 1971 and leads hikers on a diverse and beautiful path.

Trail brochures are available at the park's visitor centers or at the park office.

Relax by the fireplace in our spacious lobby

For more information on Sylvan Lake Resort call:
(605) 574-2561.

Our cabins are perfect for the entire family

At Blue Bell Lodge and Resort, you'll find the perfect hideaway in the pines ... with a western touch! Located along French Creek at the base of Mount Coolidge, amidst towering ponderosa pines, Blue Bell was built in the early 1920s by an executive at Bell Telephone. The company symbol was a blue bell, and thus the name.

ACCOMMODATIONS range from rustic cabins to new and charming hand-crafted log cabins with fireplaces and open-beamed ceilings. There are both housekeeping cabins with kitchenettes as well as sleeping cabins without cooking facilities. Fire grates are near every cabin and some cabins are available year-round!

THE TATANKA DINING ROOM is famous for down-home cooking. Dine in the comfortable western atmosphere, surrounded by old-time memorabilia. Specialties of the house are buffalo, trout and steak. The Tatanka Dining Room is open from 7 a.m. to 9 p.m. daily. The Buffalo Wallow Lounge provides an Old West saloon-style setting. Or, enjoy the outdoors from the adjoining deck or at picnic tables on the lawn. Group tours and buses are welcome.

THE WHITE BUFFALO ROOM is available for meetings and family reunions. Keep this in mind for your next family gathering or group event. Our staff will be glad to assist you with information and planning.

WESTERN CHUCKWAGON COOKOUTS are offered nightly during the summer. You'll enjoy a vehicle-drawn hayride to a Chuck Wagon cookout in a beautiful secluded canyon. Once you arrive, be sure to participate in the sing-a-long with western entertainers and enjoy a tasty steak or burger cooked and served with all the trimmings. Reservations are required, so book your spot today.

HORSE TRAIL RIDES or **PACK TRIPS** will take you on old Indian trails through some of the park's most scenic backcountry. One- or two-hour rides are available daily. Full-day and half-day rides are also available by special requests. Reservations are recommended for an Old West experience you won't soon forget. Take an overnight pack trip and camp along the trail with our Blue Bell Lodge cowboys. Enjoy campfire meals and tent camping under the stars on this western adventure. Reservations are required. For more information call (605) 255-4571.

BLUE BELL GENERAL STORE and Gift Shop is open from 7 a.m. to 9 p.m. daily during the summer months. A self-service gas station is also available.

THE BLUE BELL OUTDOOR CHAPEL, adjacent to the Lodge, holds non-denominational Sunday services at 8 a.m., June through August.

For more information on Blue Bell Lodge and Resort call:
(605) 255-4531

Fun's a cookin at our outdoor barbecues

1998 Tatanka

Legion Lake RESORT

Enjoy Legion Lake's pleasant surroundings

Located along Galena Creek, Legion Lake Resort dates back to 1913 when Custer State Park was a game preserve in the Custer State Forest. At that time, the area was leased by the American Legion Post, and thus the area's name.

Mirroring the ponderosa pines and sheer rock walls, Legion Lake offers wonderful photo opportunities. It is a natural water stop for the park's wildlife. Cottages are nestled in the pines at this lake resort.

THE LEGION LAKE DINING ROOM offers three meals served daily. The dining room offers a full-service breakfast and specializes in fresh baked breads, deli sandwiches, espresso, chicken and burgers for lunch and dinner. Take-out orders are also available. Enjoy your meal in our dining room or take in the scenery at the lake.

PADDLE BOATS, row boats, kayaks, hydro-bikes, aqua cycles and turbo prop boats are available for rent at the Legion Lake Resort. This man-made lake is also an excellent place to fish, swim or simply lie in the sun!

THE LEGION LAKE STORE and Gift Shop is open from 7 a.m. to 9 p.m. daily during the summer and offers fishing licenses, supplies, gifts and souvenirs for most vacation needs.

Boat and Bike Rentals are available at the store. Mountain bikes, paddle boats, rowboats, kayaks, hydrobikes, aqua cycles and turbo prop boats are all rented for hour, half and full day recreation adventures.

MOUNTAIN BIKES are available for rent by the day or hour at Legion Lake. Explore the back roads and mountain trails of Custer State Park. The Centennial Trail and other roads in the Legion Lake area also offer an adventure for the entire family.

TAKE A HIKE and experience the beautiful Black Hills on foot. The Centennial Trail passes right through the Legion Lake area, offering easy access for both mountain bikers and hikers. The Legion Lake Hiking Trail offers hikers a chance to view the surrounding area from a high vantage point. At the summit, a rock ledge offers panoramic views of the lake, Mount Coolidge and the southern hills.

For more information on Legion Lake Resort call:
(605) 255-4521

$1 OFF PER PERSON	$1 OFF PER PERSON	$1 OFF PER PERSON
Present this coupon for discount. Limit one coupon per party.	Present this coupon for discount. Limit one coupon per party.	Present this coupon for discount. Limit one coupon per party.
Guided Horseback Ride	**Old-fashioned Hayride & Chuck Wagon Cookout**	**Buffalo Safari Jeep Ride**
Blue Bell Stables, Hwy 87S	Blue Bell Resort, Hwy 87S	State Game Lodge, Hwy 16A
Reservations recommended: 1-605-255-4571	Reservations recommended: 1-605-255-4531	Reservations recommended: 1-605-255-4541
CUSTER STATE PARK RESORT COMPANY	CUSTER STATE PARK RESORT COMPANY	CUSTER STATE PARK RESORT COMPANY

Black Hills Playhouse

Nestled in a forested valley, next to Center Lake, the Black Hills Playhouse offers theatrical entertainment in the most lovely setting imaginable. Every year since its founding in 1946, company members from across country have gathered to offer a season of professional productions. Living in the historic CCC camp, 60 to 70 students, faculty and professional artists gather every summer to present this unique experience.

This summer's offerings include the following*:

The Trip to Bountiful
June 11-14 and 16-21

Horton Foote's award-winning, sentimental drama, starring Playhouse favorite Harriet Redden.

See How They Run
June 25-28, June 30-July 5, July 7-12.

A British farce with swift action. Rib-tickling laughter will leave you as exhausted as if you'd just run a footrace yourself.

1776 or Joseph and the Amazing Technicolor Dreamcoat
July 16-19, July 21-26, July 28-Aug. 2

Our patrons voted which of these favorite American musicals to offer after print deadline for the TATANKA, but it will be either the musical story of our nation's birth or the musical about the Biblical Joseph and his "coat of many colors."

One Flew Over the Cuckoo's Nest
Aug. 6-9 and 11-16

Ken Kesey's infamous story of McMurphy's epic battle with Nurse Rachet at an institution for mental treatment.

Nice People Dancing to Good Country Music
Aug. 20-23 and 25-30

A country comedy with a pickup truck, a bar, and a nun with Tourette's Syndrome.

*All selections subject to availability.

The Playhouse draws professional actors from around the country

Ticket prices are $19.50 for the musical and $18 to $16 for the other productions.

The Black Hills Playhouse is associated with the College of Fine Arts, University of South Dakota. This project is co-sponsored by the South Dakota Arts Council with funds from the State Legislature and the National Endowment for the Arts.

Black Hills Playhouse Cafe

And while you're in the area, be sure to stop in before or after the show for some of the best pizza, sandwiches and desserts in the Black Hills. Alcoholic beverages are also available.

The Black Hills Playhouse Cafe is open afternoons and evenings, except on Mondays when it is closed. The Black Hills Playhouse Cafe is is managed by the Custer State Park Resort Company.

Curtain Times

Evening Performances -- 8 p.m.
Matinees -- 2 p.m.

No performances on Mondays or Sunday evenings.

For more information or for reservations, call (605) 255-4141 or (605) 255-4551. Reservations are recommended. Group rates for 20 or more people are available. Season passes are available through June 15.

Explore Custer State Park!